Knowledge Spillovers and Economic Growth

NEW HORIZONS IN THE ECONOMICS OF INNOVATION

General Editor: Christopher Freeman, *Emeritus Professor of Science Policy, SPRU – Science and Technology Policy Research, University of Sussex, UK*

Technical innovation is vital to the competitive performance of firms and of nations and for the sustained growth of the world economy. The economics of innovation is an area that has expanded dramatically in recent years and this major series, edited by one of the most distinguished scholars in the field, contributes to the debate and advances in research in this most important area.

The main emphasis is on the development and application of new ideas. The series provides a forum for original research in technology, innovation systems and management, industrial organization, technological collaboration, knowledge and innovation, research and development, evolutionary theory and industrial strategy. International in its approach, the series includes some of the best theoretical and empirical work from both well-established researchers and the new generation of scholars.

Titles in the series include:

The Theory of Innovation
Entrepreneurs, Technology and Strategy
Jon Sundbo

The Emergence and Growth of Biotechnology
Experiences in Industrialised and Developing Countries
Rohini Acharya

Knowledge and Investment
The Sources of Innovation in Industry
Rinaldo Evangelista

Learning and Innovation in Economic Development
Linsu Kim

The Economics of Knowledge Production
Funding and the Structure of University Research
Aldo Geuna

Innovation and Research Policies
An International Comparative Analysis
Paul Diederen, Paul Stoneman, Otto Toivanen and Arjan Wolters

Learning and Knowledge Management in the Firm
From Knowledge Accumulation to Strategic Capabilities
Gabriela Dutrénit

Knowledge Spillovers and Economic Growth
Regional Growth Differentials across Europe
M.C.J. Caniëls

Successful Innovation
Towards a New Theory for the Management of Small and Medium Sized Enterprises
Jan Cobbenhagen

Knowledge Spillovers and Economic Growth

Regional Growth Differentials across Europe

M.C.J. Caniëls

MERIT, Maastricht and ECIS, Eindhoven, The Netherlands

NEW HORIZONS IN THE ECONOMICS OF INNOVATION

Edward Elgar
Cheltenham, UK • Northampton, MA, USA

Published by
Edward Elgar Publishing Limited
Glensanda House
Montpellier Parade
Cheltenham
Glos GL50 1UA
UK

Edward Elgar Publishing, Inc.
136 West Street
Suite 202
Northampton
Massachusetts 01060
USA

A catalogue record for this book
is available from the British Library

Library of Congress Cataloguing in Publication Data
Caniëls, Marjolein C.J., 1971–
    Knowledge spillovers and economic growth : regional growth differentials across Europe / Marjolein C.J. Caniëls.
    (New horizons in the economics of innovation)
    Includes bibliographical references and index.
    1. Europe—Economic conditions—Regional disparities. 2. Technology transfer—Europe.
    I. Title. II. Series.

HC240.C325 2000
338.94'06—dc21   99–088520

ISBN 1 84064 236 X

Printed and bound in Great Britain by Biddles Ltd, www.biddles.co.uk

Contents

List of Figures

List of Tables

For my parents

1. Introduction

1. KNOWLEDGE AND IDEAS

Many ancient civilizations knew prosperity due to important new ideas and the development of new products in the early days of their existence. From the invention of the wheel in the distant past to the discovery of antibiotics, the invention of integrated circuits and the voyages into space today, the capacity to generate new ideas and develop them into products has been generating welfare and fortune for people, since the beginning of time.

In modern economics, it is recognized that knowledge is an essential factor in generating economic growth. Knowledge and innovation are now perceived as the key ingredients for prosperity in the future. This does not exclude the importance of capital and labour as production factors; however, during the last few decades, the importance of information, knowledge and skills is emphasized.

The emergence of new information technologies and their impact on knowledge accumulation illustrate this effect. In society, an increasing use of information and communication technologies is experienced. The development of the information society is accompanied by an increasing availability of interactive multimedia services for use at home, by business or public service. Many new firms are succeeding in turning their ideas into profitable businesses with the help of these recent developments. With possibilities such as ordering products by means of the World Wide Web, a whole new market of customers can be accessed.

In economic theory, Schumpeter (1928, 1934, 1939, and 1943) laid the foundations for the modern theories of innovation. Schumpeter argued that individuals and firms in market economies have incentives to create new products and technologies. The incentive to invest in research and development is generated by the prospect that successful firms will gain a position of market power (and monopoly profits) by being the only supplier of the new product, or by being the only firm with a new cost-reducing production process. However, this market power will only be temporary, since other firms will attempt to catch up with the innovating firm and surpass it. The other firms aim to attain a new position of market power themselves to gain high profits. Over time these forces will generate waves of 'creative destruction', which will drive technological development and raise the productive capacity of the economy. Schumpeter stated that the achievement of technology was that it brought welfare for society as a whole.

In the second half of this century, the focus was directed to neo-classical models of growth. Solow (1956) and Swan (1956) laid the foundations for a whole generation of neo-classical growth models, which were centred on the idea that technological change is exogenous to the growth process (and instead focused on capital accumulation as the main endogenous source of output expansion).

A renewed emphasis on information, knowledge and skills emanated in the 1980s, which for an important part can be credited to the emergence of new growth theory. New growth theory (Romer, 1986, 1990; for an overview see Verspagen, 1992a) puts the process of technological change into the centre of economic theory by assuming knowledge to be endogenous to the production process. Endogenous growth theory views externalities, and particularly increasing returns associated with research and ideas, as the engine of economic growth. This stems from the idea that a part of the created knowledge is public, in the sense that it increases the general knowledge level in society. The research efforts of one firm do not only come to the benefit of this firm but also to the benefit of society as a whole. For example, in 1947 the transistor was invented by J. Bardeen, W.H. Brattain and W.B. Shockley, all physicists of the research staff at the Bell Telephone Laboratories (Encyclopaedia Britannica, 1998). The new knowledge was used as an input to research leading to other new technologies. The invention of the transistor led to the development of the integrated circuit (containing millions of transistors), independently by J. Kilby of Texas Instruments Incorporated in 1958 and by J. Hoemi and R. Noyce of the Fairchild Semiconductor Corporation in 1959 (Encyclopaedia Britannica, 1998). These inventions served as the foundation for the development of modern electronics. The transistor created the technology behind a whole new range of products with applications varying from military, to household, to industrial, to farming and hospital equipment. These inventions generate benefits to many people apart from the original inventors of the transistor. Thus knowledge (here in the heads of the physicists) can produce new knowledge (the transistor), some of which is used as an input to further research (integrated circuits), then the creation of still more knowledge (for example, the development of personal computers) is facilitated.

One of the implications from the new economic growth theories is that the increasing returns to knowledge may be spatially bounded. This would explain the divergence of growth rates and an unequal distribution of economic growth across space (Romer, 1986, 1990; Lucas, 1988). This leads to the main theme of this book: How can the uneven growth across geographical places be explained, and particularly, what is the role of knowledge flows in this respect? In addition, what factors influence the flow (diffusion) of knowledge, and to what extent will economic and innovative activity cluster geographically?

If new ideas are so important for growth, it is not strange that one wonders where they come from and how they are produced. Since ideas find their origin in the minds of people, one would expect that there are no spatial boundaries to ideas (Almeida and Kogut, 1996). Ideas should be independent of space. Still, there are reasons to believe that the generation of ideas and the result of ideas, namely knowledge, are locally bounded. These reasons stem from the nature of the innovative process, which can be summarized in five 'stylized facts' (Dosi, 1988; further developed by Feldman, 1994a, 1994b and Baptista and Swann, 1998). These are uncertainty, complexity, reliance on basic research, importance of learning-by-doing and cumulativeness, each of which will be discussed briefly below.

The first two stylized facts refer to the process of generating innovation out of ideas, which is a highly uncertain and complex activity. In advance, it is hardly possible to forecast whether an idea will be technically viable and whether it can be developed into a commercial success. To reduce this uncertainty people (firms) try to access information by communicating. This communication is facilitated by personal interactions, and therefore people (firms) tend to group together. This tendency can already be identified ages ago. Over the centuries, many, now famous, painters went to Italy to be taught the best techniques for painting. Since the last hundred years, every fashion designer that wants to establish a name goes to Paris. Freeman (1991) states that networks frequently tend to be localized. In addition, DeBresson and Amessa (1991, p. 370) argue that 'localised networks appear to be more durable than international strategic alliances'.

A third stylized fact of innovation is that innovation relies heavily upon sources of basic scientific knowledge such as universities and government-funded research and development (R&D)[1]. Face-to-face interaction with university scientists can make it much easier for a firm to put the information (out of scientific publications) into directly applicable knowledge (Nelson, 1989). Mansfield (1991) presents evidence that technological innovations in various industries have been based on recent academic research. Jaffe (1989) and Acs, Audretsch and Feldman (1992) have empirically shown that knowledge spillovers from university research to private firms are facilitated by geographic proximity.

---

[1] The extent to which this is the case might differ across industries.

The recent developments in information and communication technologies might lead to the belief that in these days knowledge is freely available to everyone. However, it is not knowledge but rather information that is freely available. Dasgupta and David (1993, p. 9) describe the distinction between knowledge and information: information is 'knowledge reduced and converted into messages that can be easily communicated among decision agents'. Audretsch and Feldman (1996) argue that although the cost of transmitting information may be invariant to distance, presumably the cost of transmitting knowledge rises with distance. Therefore, proximity and location play an essential role in the transmission of knowledge. In addition, Pavitt (1987) argues that *new* technological knowledge is informal and uncodified in its nature. Therefore, this new knowledge should flow locally more easily than over great distances. The underlying idea is that knowledge can be learned through practice. Possibilities for learning-by-doing and learning-by-using come from direct contacts with competitors, customers, suppliers and providers of services (Von Hippel, 1988, 1994). This explains the fourth stylized fact of innovation.

Finally, innovative activity is cumulative in its nature. This means that new innovations build upon scientific knowledge generated by previous innovations. The concept of 'cumulativeness' is also highly relevant in the context of geographic clustering. Breschi (1995) and Malerba and Orsenigo (1995) show that cumulativeness of innovative activity plays a key role in shaping the geographical pattern of innovative activity. The underlying idea is that geographic areas (regions) that have accumulated high levels of innovative activity have assembled information that facilitates the generation of new innovations (Grossman and Helpman, 1992).

Over the last years, there has been a growing interest in the literature concerning topics associated with the spatial dimension of economic growth and technological change. The literature exposes a wide variety of contributions on the location of production. To name a few, Kozul-Wright and Rowthorn (1998) study the geographic unevenness induced by the location of multinational firms. Lall (1998) reveals the unevenness in patterns of trade and industry location in developing countries. Amiti (1998) shows that there is an increasing concentration of industries in Western Europe, whereas Hanson (1998) focuses on the North American Free Trade Area and studies the geographic concentrated pattern of industrial location. Chapter 8 of this book will explore the location of industries within European regions.

Next to these studies, there is a growing literature on agglomeration and the geography of knowledge (Audretsch, 1998; Feldman and Audretsch, 1999) and new economic geography (Krugman, 1991, 1998). This stream in the literature takes geographical advantages of some areas as endogenously determined by the ease of interaction among economic agents.

Many case studies were carried out on the effects of innovative milieus, technology or industrial districts and scientific or technology parks. Among these studies on local systems of innovation are Dorfman (1983) with a study on the Route 128, Saxenian (1985) on Silicon Valley, Scott (1988) on Orange County and Stohr (1986) on regional innovation complexes.

In addition, a lot of empirical and econometric literature tries to measure the extent and importance of regional spillovers in different ways: Jaffe (1989), Jaffe et al (1993), Feldman (1994a), Audretsch (1995), Audretsch and Feldman (1996) and Breschi (1995). These studies emphasize the advantages of geographical proximity for receiving knowledge spillovers. However, the underlying mechanisms by which knowledge spillovers take place are not well understood yet. This book will argue that, next to geographic proximity, technological proximity to an economically active region is important for knowledge spillovers. Furthermore, the impact of localized knowledge spillovers on regional growth rates is analysed.

2. AIM OF THE BOOK AND LIMITATIONS

The aim of this book is to broaden the understanding of knowledge spillovers (across space) in general and the factors that have an influence on knowledge spillovers in particular. Furthermore, the influence of locally bounded knowledge spillovers on growth across regions is analysed. The focus will be on regional knowledge spillovers, instead of spillovers on a country level. The reason for adopting a regional view is that this allows us to analyse the influence of space, which would not be possible by considering countries only. A region comprises a geographic area that is far smaller than a country, therefore regional analysis can give a better view on localized spillovers than an analysis at the country level.

With this focus on regions, the book links up with the renewed interest in regions in the event of a united Europe. On the one hand, European integration increases the awareness of the separate cultures within Europe. People are fearful of losing their identity and focus on their regional roots. On the other hand, there is an economic concern, specifically with regions. Reinforcing the unity of economies by reducing (economic) disparities among the regions is among the goals written down in the Treaty of Rome. This has served as a basis for setting up a policy of support for regional development.

Several mechanisms can be distinguished by which research efforts generate spillovers. In this book, we will concentrate on knowledge spillovers. Knowledge spillovers are intellectual gains by exchange of information for which no direct compensation to the producer of the knowledge is given or for which less compensation is given than the value of the knowledge. Knowledge spillovers can be embodied or disembodied (see Chapter 2). Other forms of spillovers are 'market spillovers' and 'network spillovers' (Jaffe, 1996). Market spillovers capture the welfare gain for the consumers associated with improved products (consumer surplus). Network spillovers occur as the value for a participant in, for example, a research project lies in an increasing number of participants. Then each firm that decides to participate creates a positive externality to potential participants because it increases the probability that enough parties are involved to make the research project successful.

The term 'knowledge diffusion' reflects a much broader concept. It comprises the transfer of knowledge over time and space via all conceivable ways, one of which is diffusion by knowledge spillovers. Next to knowledge diffusion (or technology transfer), we can distinguish the diffusion of innovations. The vast amount of literature on this topic (for a survey see Metcalfe (1988)) is mainly concerned with the changes in economic significance over time of a new technology. Section 3 in Chapter 2 partly deals with the diffusion of innovations.

3. OUTLINE OF THE BOOK

The rest of this book is set out as follows. Chapters 2 and 3 are concerned with the description of the literature on diffusion of knowledge and provides a methodological framework. Chapter 2 presents a (selective) overview of the literature. It reviews several strands starting with neo-classical economics and ending with recent contributions to the literature with respect to regional economics. (The remainder of the book will follow the line set out by recent publications in this field emphasis lying on diffusion over space.) Chapter 3 introduces evolutionary thinking as setting the methodological framework for this book. The Goodwin model is brought forward as a prototype model of economic evolution.

Chapters 4 to 6 of the book focus on analysing the influence of knowledge spillovers on regional gaps. They are devoted to setting up a model that gives an impression of these effects. The implications of the model are explored by means of simulation techniques. The aim of Chapter 4 is to integrate spatial issues as brought forward in Chapter 2 into technology gap models. The absence of space as an explaining factor in technology gap models is addressed in this chapter by extending a simple technology gap model with the concept of geographical distance. The model is constructed in a way that is applicable to a multitude of regions. Chapter 5 reviews the simulations carried out to analyse the workings of the model. Chapter 6 develops a multi-country model, in which interregional knowledge spillovers determine the growth of regions. By simulations, the effect of several parameters such as learning capability and exogenous knowledge generation on disparity is analysed under different circumstances. With the help of this model, a monetary union can be compared to a system of flexible exchange rates, with respect to their influence on disparity. In addition, the effect of barriers to knowledge spillovers can be analysed in the sense that cross-border knowledge flows are hampered compared to inter-country flows.

Finally, Chapters 7 and 8 deal with the current situation in Europe, using empirical analyses to demonstrate regional gaps and differences in economic and innovative activity across regions. The model developed in Chapters 4 and 6 is related to the present situation in Europe. Chapter 7 focuses on data on Gross Domestic Product (GDP) and the inputs of innovation, and sheds light on the geographical distribution of growth and knowledge across European regions. The focus is on exploring the extent to which the patterns generated by the model presented earlier resemble the ones empirically observed. Chapter 8 takes more distance from the model in that it tries to give a more detailed view on the present situation within Europe without focusing too much on the expectations based on the model. To this end the chapter explores data on manufacturing value added and patents in order to direct attention to sector differences (which were assumed to be absent in the model).

Chapter 9 concludes the book by summarizing the results and offering some concluding remarks. The implications for policy are explored and directions for future research pointed out.

2. Knowledge and Location

Over the years, a lot of attention has been paid to explaining regional differences in economic growth. Less attention was directed towards the issue of knowledge diffusion, at least by economists. This was mainly due to the enormous impact of neo-classical theory in all segments of economic theory. Under the neo-classical model, technology was assumed to spread immediately and be 'under competition available to all' (Borts and Stein, 1964, p. 8). In the neo-classical line of reasoning, it can be argued that knowledge is easily codifiable in blueprints, patents, and so on. Therefore, it can be accessed easily everywhere, that is to say, knowledge spreads immediately and technology gaps between geographical locations do not exist.

Today, information communication has led to a substantial increase in the spread of information. Features such as electronic mail, the worldwide web and newsgroups enable people to get access to information all over the world in a few seconds. However, to argue that all knowledge spreads immediately, as in the neo-classical view, would be wrong. Now, more than ever, the impact of tacit knowledge becomes visible. Tacit knowledge is knowledge that is embedded in persons, in the specific skills people have acquired over time. A characteristic of tacit knowledge is that it is very difficult, if not impossible, to document and diffuse (Cowan and Foray, 1997). The main way to diffuse this kind of knowledge is by learning or face-to-face contact. Therefore, there is an important difference between knowledge and information. Whereas information can be easily codified and is available at low cost invariant to distance, knowledge is tacit in its nature. The cost of transmitting (tacit) knowledge rises with distance (Audretsch, 1998).

When applying these insights to regional economics, it becomes clear that the traditional neo-classical view is invalid. Tacit knowledge will be kept in firms, so knowledge will stay with one geographical location and not diffuse easily. Therefore, technology gaps between regions may persist. The only knowledge that does diffuse is the kind of knowledge that provides others with general information but not specific details. It is like the cook who gives you the ingredients but not the recipe to make a delicious meal.

In the literature, the impact of tacit knowledge was acknowledged when the neo-classical model was applied to regional economics. Only then the assumption about technology became severely criticized. The question that was raised by economists was whether alternative models could explain reality better by paying more attention to the diffusion of knowledge. In course of time, various alternative models were developed, which assumed knowledge to spread imperfectly, or not at all. In other words, the absence of technology gaps between regions, which was assumed by neo-classical economists, was questioned severely.

Figure 2.1: Schematic overview of the various streams in the literature

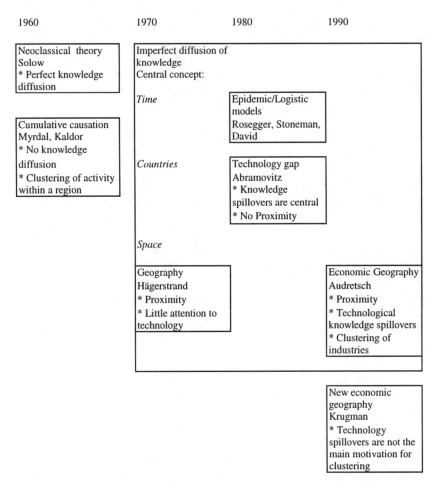

Later on, a strand in economic geography argued that proximity and location are very important in the transmission of knowledge. It is easier to transmit knowledge over short than over large distances. Therefore, knowledge externalities can be reaped by a location within a cluster of firms or nearby universities or research centres.

Figure 2.1 gives a schematic overview of the various streams in the literature. The remainder of this chapter will go into more detail about how the various streams of research incorporated knowledge diffusion over regions. First, in Section 1, the regional neo-classical growth theory will be discussed, which assumed knowledge to be perfectly mobile. Another extreme is to assume complete immobility of knowledge, that is to say, technology stays within one region and therefore comes to the benefit of only this region. This assumption was made in cumulative causation models, which will be discussed in Section 2. Section 3 discusses a third class of models, which assume knowledge to spread slowly. The speed and sequence of diffusion depend on various factors in this model.

1. NEO-CLASSICAL THEORY FROM A REGIONAL PERSPECTIVE

The neo-classical growth model serves as the basic tool for understanding the growth process in advanced countries and has been applied in empirical studies of the sources of economic growth. Since the 1960s, many regional economists have tried to disaggregate the neo-classical growth model into a regional growth model. Borts (1960) can be noted as the first case of a regional neo-classical growth model. In his model the following assumptions were made: (i) the total supply of labour available to all regions together is fixed. The only way in which one region may employ more labour is through immigration from other regions; (ii) a single homogeneous output is produced in each region; (iii) there are zero transport costs between regions, so that the price of output is uniform; (iv) there are zero costs of converting output into capital goods; (v) the same production function exists in each region, being homogeneous of degree one in the inputs labour and capital, so technical knowledge is under competition available to all and diffusion is immediate.

It should be emphasized that the value of this traditional neo-classical regional growth model depends heavily on the underlying assumptions, which are very unrealistic and in some cases even incompatible with the regional setting (Richardson, 1973, 1978a, 1978b). The assumption perhaps most commonly questioned as to its realism in a regional model was that of immediate diffusion of knowledge. It was considered hard to maintain this assumption, taking into account the distance between the place of invention/innovation and the rest of the country. The issues of space and distance (and also the time needed to bridge the distance) are completely ignored. When introducing regions in the model, many economists argued, the concepts of space and distance needed to be acknowledged, because only these concepts could bring a full understanding of the forces behind the differences in growth between regions (or nations when considering a more aggregated view) (Richardson, 1973). Besides labour and capital, for which the assumption of mobility is perhaps more appropriate[2], the neo-classical model should also have paid attention to knowledge. It is this 'omission' that has come to be seen as the main limitation of the early neo-classical regional growth model.

Regarding growth rate differentials, the neo-classical model, at least in its unaltered form, predicts convergence[3]. In the pure aggregate neo-classical model, it can be shown that when differences in the growth rate of output between countries exist, these will disappear under the influence of differential capital accumulation, which can be generated by investments or by movements of production factors. When capital accumulation takes place through movements of production factors, as assumed in most of the regional literature, the process is as follows. Under the usual assumption of decreasing marginal returns to production factors, it can be shown that the return to capital (marginal product of capital) is an inverse function of the capital-labour ratio, and the wage rate (marginal product of labour) is a direct function of the capital labour ratio. Therefore, given identical production functions in all countries and capital accumulation through factor movements, labour will flow from low- to high-wage countries, and capital will flow in the opposite direction. These flows will continue until all differences in the growth rate of output have disappeared (Richardson, 1973, 1978a, 1978b), and the long-run steady state and exogenously determined growth rates are reached (Barro and Sala-i-Martin, 1991). As Barro (1991) and Barro and Sala-i-Martin (1991, 1992a and b) have demonstrated, the further economies are from the steady state position, the faster they tend to converge towards this long-run steady state[4].

Thus, applying this aggregated neo-classical view to regional models, a high capital/labour ratio in a region ~ caused by a difference in factor

---

[2] Although capital is much more mobile than labour (Richardson, 1973).

[3] As will be noticed in subsequent paragraphs, adjustment or manipulation of the assumptions of the neo-classical model can lead to other outcomes. In addition, convergence of levels of GDP per capita is conditional on savings rates (Barro and Sala-i-Martin, 1995).

[4] In the long-run steady state of a neo-classical growth model, the growth rate of output is equal to the growth rate of capital. A further description of the dynamics of the neo-classical model is given by Solow (1970), Mankiw, Romer, Weil (1992) or Barro and Sala-i-Martin (1995).

endowments ~ will lead to high wages and low rates of return to capital. Given identical production functions in all regions, this causes an inflow of labour and an outflow of capital in this region. These flows continue until factor returns are equalized in each region, thus, until the capital/labour ratio is brought back to its equilibrium value and the aggregate economy is in a steady state. This regional process will cause regional per capita income levels to converge, if at least certain additional assumptions are met (such as equal labour participation rates, property income distributed among regions in proportion to population) (Richardson, 1978a).

Unfortunately, it has been impossible to test the predictions of the neo-classical model properly, because of a lack of usable regional capital stock and capital yield data. The tests that were carried out have merely investigated whether convergence in regional per capita income levels takes place (Richardson, 1978a)[5]. The results from these tests were put forward as giving support to the following hypotheses of the neo-classical model: (i) 'the return to capital is inversely related to regional capital-labour ratios', and (ii) 'net capital flows are a function of differentials in the inter-regional rates of return on capital' (Richardson, 1978a, p. 27). However, obviously, results of empirical tests on convergence in per capita income levels only indirectly support these hypotheses and thereby the neo-classical model.

In addition, empirical tests indicated different outcomes (convergence or divergence) depending on the country or the period under concern. Since Borts (1960), many regional economists have adjusted the neo-classical assumptions in order to make the model more realistic. In due course, every single assumption has been changed and manipulated in order to reflect reality better. By relaxing some of these assumptions, it was possible to achieve completely different outcomes of the model, in particular to explain divergence rather than convergence. However, alternative models, like the cumulative causation model[6], were also capable of generating divergence results. This obviously raised the question of whether an alternative, non-neo-classical model would not be more feasible to explain the observed outcomes (Richardson, 1973, 1978a, 1978b). This strong critique applies to the early models (1960-1970) in the neo-classical tradition. Later, many models have

---

[5] See for instance recent tests carried out by Barro and Sala-i-Martin (1991, 1992a and b). Barro and Sala-i-Martin (1991) show patterns of convergence in regional per capita income levels across 73 regions of Western Europe since 1950. In their 1992(a) study, they present evidence for the hypothesis of convergence in regional per capita incomes across the 48 contiguous US states. The authors explicitly state that their tests give evidence for the hypothesis that poor regions grow faster than rich ones (β-convergence), or, the hypothesis of convergence in the levels of per capita income and product.

[6] See next paragraph.

been developed in this tradition that account for market imperfections in a sophisticated way.

In the same way, adjustments were made to incorporate space and distance in a neo-classical growth model. However,

> Although the neo-classical model may be modified or manipulated to provide a reasonable replication of the regional growth process, the spatial aspects of regional analysis reveal the limitation of the basic neo-classical model. The neo-classical growth analyst may choose to remain faithful to his traditional methodology, but alternative frameworks can more easily cope with the complication of space (Richardson, 1978b, p. 143).

To come back to the argument made in the beginning of this section, the first step towards greater realism with respect to space and distance would be to alter the reasoning concerning knowledge diffusion. The neo-classical way of regarding knowledge diffusion as immediate should be replaced by an alternative idea like slow diffusion or (as in the next section) no diffusion at all.

2. CUMULATIVE CAUSATION

This section will outline two 'objections' to the traditional neo-classical growth theory discussed by Kaldor (1970, 1975). Firstly, Kaldor states that the traditional neo-classical theory excessively emphasizes the importance of resource allocation and the idea that differences in resource endowments between regions explain differences in regional growth rates. Here, resource endowments consist of endowments of capital, in which capital means both 'the plant and machinery, and human skills, resulting from education' (Kaldor, 1970, p. 339). Secondly, he objects to the fact that the neo-classical model assumes constant returns to scale, which should be replaced by increasing returns to scale. According to Kaldor (1970, 1975), technology is immobile. By elaborating these two points in the subsequent paragraphs, the cumulative causation model will be explained.

With regard to his first objection to the neo-classical framework, Kaldor (1970, 1975) stresses that differences in resource endowments do not explain why industries are located in certain regions and not in other regions. He argues that to a certain extent, the neo-classical reasoning is correct, namely in the case of 'land-based' activities, which depend on climatic and geological factors. However, with respect to industrial activities, one cannot attribute the differences in development among regions to differences in resource endowments. Differences in resource endowments originate from differences in economic growth, but they also *cause* economic growth (Kaldor, 1970). These two effects cannot be separated. In other words, the resources for manufacturing are endogenous, in contrast to the exogenously determined resources for land-based activities. As Kaldor puts it: 'It is as sensible ~ or perhaps more sensible ~ to say that capital accumulation results from economic development as that it is a cause of development' (Kaldor, 1970, p. 339). The idea that output growth causes productivity growth is often referred to as the *Verdoorn-Kaldor law*[7]. According to Kaldor (1970), it is this relationship that could contribute to the explanation of divergent growth of regions.

According to the Verdoorn-Kaldor law, output growth causes growth of productivity, because of static and dynamic economies of scale. Economies of scale can be divided into two groups. First, economies resulting from large-scale production, referred to as static economies of scale, such as for instance the further division of labour at the individual plant level. A second group of economies of scale originates from 'the insight that the spatial concentration of economic activity can produce externalities' (Malecki and Varaiya, 1986). This group, referred to as dynamic economies of scale, consists of cumulative advantages that originate from the growth of the industry itself, like learning-by-doing and 'the development of skill and know-how; the opportunities for easy communication of ideas and experience; the opportunity of ever-increasing differentiation of processes and of specialisation in human activities' (Kaldor, 1970, p. 340).

A related concept, stemming more explicitly from the field of regional studies, is that of *agglomeration economies*, which partly overlaps with the previous idea. The general idea behind agglomeration economies is that the environment of the firm has an influence on the output of the firm. A spatial concentration of economic activity and people in the environment of a certain firm generates positive effects on the productivity of this firm, because, for instance, the opportunity for communication of ideas and experience is much larger. In this respect, also, the presence of a research institute or a university could generate positive external effects for the firm[8]. In short, agglomeration

---

[7] According to the Verdoorn law (Verdoorn, 1949), a positive relation exists between the growth of productivity, measured by the rate of growth of output per employee, and the growth rate of employment. Later, Kaldor (1967) modified this reasoning by replacing employment growth by output growth. The resulting relationship became known as the Verdoorn-Kaldor law.

[8] It should be noted that the concept of growth poles as put forward by regional economists like Perroux (1955) and Boudeville (1966) is different from that of agglomeration economies. As Richardson (1978) explains clearly, 'agglomeration economies mean the economies inducing people and activities to cluster together, not the *effects* of agglomeration. Although some agglomeration economies are size related, for example, the provision of high-level urban services requiring a large population threshold, increasing size is more the result than a cause of

economies are everything that induces people and economic activities to cluster together (Richardson, 1978a).

In a simple model, Malecki and Varaiya (1986) represent agglomeration economies by letting output be determined by a Cobb-Douglas equation which is multiplied by an additional term, denoted by D^a. The variable D represents the effects of urban density or concentration on output. If the parameter a is positive, it indicates agglomeration economies. On the other hand, if a is negative, this would indicate congestion effects. From their simple model it can easily be seen that 'agglomeration economies imply that the same capital equipment and labour in a plant operating in a larger urban environment will produce more than the plant in a smaller urban environment' (Malecki and Varaiya, 1986, p. 632).

In the regional literature, a specific interpretation is given to the Verdoorn-Kaldor law. For this law to be true, according to regional economists, it has to be assumed that 'the increased investment resulting from higher growth in a region is located in the same region' (Malecki and Varaiya, 1986, p. 632), that is to say, because a certain region experiences higher growth, investment in the same region grows. Part of the investment will be devoted to research and development (R&D). The benefits of this increased R&D-investment are assumed to be reaped only in this very same region, thus only in this region productivity grows. This in turn will cause a rise in the output of the region, that is to say, the region will experience growth. In this process, there is no diffusion of technology at all. The benefits of technical progress stay within the region that experiences the benefits of an increased investment, and therefore only this region shows an increase in productivity. This reasoning (referred to as *the principle of circular and cumulative causation*, Myrdal, 1957) explains why differences in productivity among regions may be persistent rather than a transitory state, as in the neo-classical model[9]. As Kaldor (1970, p. 340) argues, the principle of circular and cumulative

---

agglomeration economies' (Richardson, 1978a, p. 156). Thus, the evolution of a growth pole is an effect of agglomeration economies. It is beyond the scope of this section to discuss the growth pole theory of for example Perroux and Boudeville more explicitly. However, Kaldor (1975) also acknowledges the development of growth poles when he argues that 'industrial development tends to get polarized in certain 'growth points' or in 'success areas', which become areas of vast immigration from surrounding centers or from more distant areas, unless this is prevented by political obstacles' (Kaldor, 1975, p. 356).

[9] Dixon and Thirlwall (1975) presented a model based on the Verdoorn law and the principle of cumulative causation. Their model explains persistent differences in (regional) growth rates. The idea is that a region can experience an exogenous shock that increases its growth rate. Via Verdoorn's law productivity growth is increased as well. In turn, exports are positively influenced which stimulates economic growth. This self-reinforcing system will damp down over time (under certain parameter values); the growth rate differential will remain, however.

causation 'is nothing else but the existence of increasing returns to scale in processing activities'.

Of course, by assuming technology to be completely immobile, as opposed to the neo-classical view of complete mobility, Kaldor advocates another extreme and therefore unrealistic assumption. A theory based on imperfect mobility and slow diffusion of technology might approach reality much better. The next section will introduce some theories that stress this point of view.

3. IMPERFECT DIFFUSION

How do innovations diffuse over space? Traditional diffusion theory does not consider this question, but instead focuses on diffusion over time. Inspired by natural sciences (like epidemiology) and sociological thinking (with concepts like 'spread by contact'), economists devoted attention to the study of S-shaped curves as a representation of the diffusion of knowledge over time. A number of approaches are concerned with diffusion over time. Firstly, the epidemic model, in which diffusion was thought to have the same characteristics as the spread of an epidemic disease. During the early stages of the process the spread of innovation will be slow, because the probability of one adopter contacting a potential adopter is still low. However, this probability will increase over time. Halfway through the process a breakpoint occurs; due to the limited population of potential adopters the probability will decline again, until the saturation point is approached (the population has run out of potential adopters, that is to say, every adopter who would want to adopt the innovation has adopted it) (Rosegger, 1980). This process can be described by a logistic diffusion curve.

The epidemic model has some drawbacks, mainly related to the exogenous nature of its explanation, which led to a set of improved models. In the probit model of David (1975), it was recognized that the group of adopters of an innovation is not homogeneous. There may be a difference in the profitability of adoption of a specific innovation among firms. In David's model the adoption of the innovation will be profitable only for firms above a given size. He states that adoption of a mechanical reaper is profitable for a farm i at time t if:

$$w_t(L_{it}^{Old} - L_{it}^{New}) \geq p_{it}^{New} \tag{1.1}$$

where w denotes the wage rate, L points to the labour requirements and p is the average annual cost of a reaping method. The superscripts *Old* and *New* point to the old (manual) method of reaping and the new (mechanical) method respectively. He assumes that there are no economies of scale in either method and therefore the labour requirements are a linear function of the size of the farm S:

$$L_{it}^{Old} = a_1 S_{it}$$
(1.2)

$$L_{it}^{New} = a_2 S_{it}.$$
(1.3)

where a_1 and a_2 are positive constants for which it holds that $a_1 > a_2$. The condition for profitable adoption is then:

$$S_{it} \geq \frac{p_{it}^{New}}{w_t} \frac{1}{a_1 - a_2}.$$
(1.4)

It is assumed that not all farms fulfil this condition at the time the mechanical reapers are first introduced, therefore diffusion of the innovation is not instantaneous. Adoption of the new technology happens only when the farms increase in size, the average annual costs of reapers (p^{New}) declines relative to the wage rate and/or the reapers are improved technologically (which would lead to a decrease in a_2). Thus, diffusion is conditional on, among other things, the characteristics of the adopters, which can change over time.

Another important flaw of the epidemic model is the neglect of the supply side. For the diffusion of an innovation it is essential that an innovation will be implemented and, therefore, that it is profitable to manufacture products embodying the innovation (Coombs, Saviotti and Walsh, 1987). In order to correct this deficiency, several models were developed, for example, Stoneman (1983, 1984) and Metcalfe (1981).

3.1 Technology gaps: diffusion over countries

After some early publications such as Gerschenkron (1962) and Abramovitz (1979), research on technology diffusion over countries was deepened during the 1980s. Economists started to realize the importance of diffusion over countries for the falsification of the assumption of perfect knowledge mobility, as used in the traditional neo-classical theory. As an alternative to the neo-classical model of (regional) growth, the technology gap approach was introduced. Within this approach the concepts of 'catching up' and 'falling behind' play an important role. By means of these concepts, the technology gap approach attempts to give an explanation for the differences in productivity growth rates between countries (or regions).

In contrast to the theory set out by Siebert (1969)[10], which assumes polarization, the catch-up analysis in its simplest form is based on the idea that eventually, per capita income levels and growth rates will show a tendency to converge. However, within the technology gap literature a variety of ideas is brought forward with respect to the specific way convergence is perceived. These will be discussed in the following.

The idea that underlies the technology gap approach is that a technological difference between countries (or regions) 'opens up the possibility for countries at a lower level of economic and technological development to catch up by imitating the more productive technologies of the leader country' (Fagerberg, 1988, p. 439). Abramovitz (1986) argues that this catching-up process is conditional upon some specific factors, referred to as social capability and technological congruence. According to Abramovitz, a country that is technologically backward but socially advanced has a large potential for rapid growth. If this country also possesses the means to realize this potential for catch-up, it will be able to converge towards the technological leader[11].

As stated above, there are two factors that influence the potential for catch-up. The first one, referred to as social capability[12], describes all the factors that facilitate the imitation of a technology, or the implementation of technology spillovers (Abramovitz, 1986). Social capability 'relates to factors such as education, an appropriate financial system, labour market relations etc.' (Fagerberg, Verspagen, von Tunzelman, 1994, p. 5). The second factor that determines the extent to which a country (or region) has a potential for catch-up is called technological congruence. This concerns the extent to which the country is technologically near the leader country, that is, how far it is able to apply the technical features from the new knowledge. As Fagerberg, Verspagen, von Tunzelman state, technological congruence is 'referring to the assumption that technological progress depends on leader-country characteristics, and that backward countries ~ to implement leader-country technologies ~ need to emulate some of these characteristics' (Fagerberg, Verspagen, von Tunzelman, 1994, p. 5).

---

[10] See Section 3.2 of this chapter.

[11] Verspagen (1991) argues that the realization of catch-up will close the technological gap between countries only to a certain extent. To establish a complete closure of the technological gap the research and development efforts in the backward country should be raised (post catching up).

[12] Ohkawa and Rosovsky (1973) first introduced the term 'social capability'. With this term they denoted 'those factors constituting a country's ability to import or engage in technological and organizational progress' (Ohkawa and Rosovsky, 1973, p. 212).

The assumed convergence process ~ which is conditional on social capability and technological congruence ~ will generate a situation in which the technologically backward countries (the followers) catch up to a large extent with the technologically more advanced countries (the leaders). Thus, at the end of this process, the two groups of countries (regions) have converged and only one large group of countries (regions) with roughly identical technology (and the same rate of growth) will result.

Another idea with respect to catch-up was proposed in a theoretical study by Ames and Rosenberg (1963). They introduce the idea that a backward country can surpass the leader country. Thus, after some time the followers will not only catch up with the leader countries (or regions), but even take over the lead. So the old leaders have become followers. This situation will last for some time and then the group of followers will again take over from the leaders. This process will continue, merely because both groups will expose innovation and imitation qualities. So an interplay between these two forces exists: 'innovation, which tends to increase economic and techno-logical differences between countries, and imitation or diffusion, which tends to reduce them' (Fagerberg, 1988, p. 439). 'In general, the outcome of the international process of innovation and diffusion ... is uncertain. The process may generate a pattern where countries follow diverging trends, as well as a pattern where countries converge towards a common mean' (Fagerberg, 1988, p. 439).

In addition to these theoretical studies, empirical tests were carried out searching for convergence or divergence. Among the large range of tests two groups can be distinguished. First, tests which aimed at demonstrating simple global convergence. Second, tests which tried to distinguish between groups of countries, where convergence occurs within a group but not between the groups.

Baumol (1986) uses data for the period 1870-1978 (provided mainly by Maddison (1982)) to show convergence of productivities of sixteen industrialized countries. De Long (1988) provided a critical comment on this study. His main remark is that 'Baumol's regression uses an *ex post* sample of countries that are now rich and have successfully developed' (De Long, 1988, p. 1138). This cannot provide a rightful basis for making conclusions about convergence, because the sample consists of only those countries that have converged, that is, the sample of Baumol is biased. De Long establishes a new (unbiased) sample that consists of 22 countries that all possessed the potential to converge in 1870. The criterion for constructing this sample was the level of income for several countries in 1870. De Long finds no convergence, but rather some evidence for divergence.

In a reply to this comment Baumol, Blackman and Wolff (1989) repeat their tests based on an *ex ante* sample, and they conclude that the results of several tests indicate that divergence exists up to 1860. After that, small convergence groups appear which enlarge over time, but never get that large to include the whole 22 countries of De Long.

Another line of research was developed somewhat later by authors like Durlauf and Johnson (1992), who carried out empirical tests that indicated multi-group convergence. The central idea is that at the end of the convergence process there will be two (or more) groups of countries, identified by specific characteristics. One group will not catch up with the other; however, the countries *within* a group show convergence. This phenomenon is called local convergence.

Next to empirical studies on convergence and divergence, several empirical studies have been undertaken to quantify the diffusion of knowledge by measuring knowledge spillovers across countries. Griliches (1979) made a distinction between two kinds of technology spillovers. The first sort is composed of spillovers that are embodied within products. The second sort of spillovers is pure knowledge spillovers. These represent the spillovers that are not embodied in products but flow from one person to another on conferences, fairs, business meetings, and so on. One important difference with rent spillovers is that pure knowledge spillovers are intellectual gains by exchange of information for which the producer of the knowledge is not paid directly. Technology gap literature focuses on pure knowledge spillovers. A few contributions (based on new growth theory) are devoted to international knowledge spillovers of a disembodied kind. Each of these studies uses an index to measure the intensity of spillovers. Park (1995) applies the idea of 'technological closeness'[13] to international knowledge spillovers. He uses a similarity in R&D across countries as an indicator of who the technological neighbours are. His research takes sector differences into account, since he assumes that: 'each research sector in a country benefits most from research conducted in the same sector abroad and less from different sectors', (Park, 1995, p. 574). He finds that productivity growth and R&D investments in other countries are affected by knowledge spillovers. Coe and Helpman (1995) use bilateral trade flows as a measure for the intensity of spillovers. They assume that a country receives more spillovers from countries from which it imports relatively more goods and

---

[13] Jaffe (1989) introduced this term in a study that was directed at knowledge flows between firms. Technological closeness stands for a weight to measure the fraction of the R&D efforts of a knowledge-spilling entity in the total pool of knowledge available to the knowledge-receiving entity.

services. Cumulative R&D expenditure is used as a proxy for the knowledge stock of a country. They find that there are significant effects of international R&D spillovers on total factor productivity and labour productivity growth.

3.2 Diffusion over space

As argued above, until the 1970s, with the exception of Siebert (1969), the economic literature paid attention to diffusion of knowledge over time and not over space. Spatial diffusion of knowledge was mainly considered by economic geographers and not by regional economists. As was argued by geographers, 'diffusion of innovation over space occurs according to predictable patterns which fail ... to penetrate all conceivable locations' (Richardson, 1973, p. 113). Siebert (1969) attempted to incorporate technology creation, application and spread into a neo-classical growth model. The main contribution of Siebert to economic thinking was that he assumed technology not to be perfectly mobile, but to diffuse slowly over time and space. This section will discuss the viewpoint of the geographers as well as the contribution of Siebert to this field in economics.

At the beginning of the 1970s, economic geographers had proposed the idea of diffusion of knowledge over space. The central idea is that inventions can take place everywhere across space, but that they diffuse along specific paths. Broadly, a distinction between two types of diffusion process can be made.

First, the general spatial diffusion model. The assumption was made that economic growth, usually in the form of innovations, would spread throughout a growth centre's hinterland and to 'lower order' cities, (for example, Darwent, 1969; Moseley, 1974; Todd, 1974; Malecki, 1983). Thus, innovations were expected to spread among regions from one region to its neighbours and so on. This model is mainly used to study diffusion processes in underdeveloped regions. Empirical observation of undeveloped societies shows such a typical pattern with respect to diffusion of innovation. In most cases, implementation of inventions takes place in the spatial surroundings of the original innovation centre. After the innovation has been implemented in a certain spatial neighbourhood of this innovation centre, the diffusion process halts. Therefore, smaller urban centres are not reached. 'There is very little penetration into smaller urban centres and rural areas, especially when these are isolated from the main innovation centre' (Richardson, 1973, p. 126).

The contrary occurs in a hierarchical system of diffusion. This second type of diffusion process advocates that innovations spread from the place of invention to other large centres in the economy. As time passes the innovation will also reach hierarchically lower urban centres. One argument for this reasoning was given by Richardson (1978b): 'Larger cities are more likely to be receptive to innovations because of disproportionate concentration there of the innovation adopting elite (technologists, managers and R&D specialists), a more favourable social structure and the location there of decision-making centres of large corporations.' In this type of diffusion model, the most important factor determining the timing and rate of acceptance of a new technology was thought to be the region size (measured by population), because it represents the spatial concentration of entrepreneurs and industry as well as market potential (Brown, 1981, see Malecki and Varaiya, 1986). This theory can be summarized in the hypothesis that 'innovations spread among regions in a sequence that begins with larger, or more populous, regions and only later includes smaller regions' (Malecki and Varaiya, 1986, p. 634). This form of diffusion is mainly seen in developed countries.

However, reality does not support such a strict division between spatial and hierarchical models. It frequently occurs that in the beginning of the diffusion process the hierarchical model dominates, which with the passing of time is taken over by the spatial diffusion process. Hägerstrand (1966, p. 40) states that 'the point of introduction in a new country is its primate city; sometimes some other metropolis. Then centres next in rank follow. Soon, however, this order is broken up and replaced by one where the neighbourhood effect dominates over pure size succession.' Thus, at first an innovation spreads depending on the size of the city or region (measured by the population); after a short period diffusion proceeds depending on the proximity of potential buyers. The period until the spatial diffusion process takes over from the hierarchical diffusion process might be very short. For example, the place of introduction of a new product will be most often in a metropolitan city, because of hierarchical diffusion. After this first introduction, diffusion will, in all likelihood, develop simultaneously through the hierarchical line as well as spatially. The logic behind hierarchical diffusion in this case would be that the economic risks are less in a larger potential market. However, the argument of spatial diffusion would be that the innovation might be imitated more easily by proximate places which would have a higher probability of exposure to it (Robson, 1973).

In his study, Siebert (1969) points out that there are other factors, apart from a high population density and geographic proximity, which have an influence on the spread of knowledge. In his analysis, he focuses on three main factors that influence the mobility of knowledge and determine the specialization of a region.

Siebert concentrates his analysis on three basic ingredients for a perfect flow of knowledge, and shows that every ingredient comprises imperfections. For a perfect transfer of knowledge about new inventions between regions a sender, a receiver and a system of communication are required. Each of these three factors can exhibit flaws that slow down the speed of knowledge transfer. First, with respect to the senders of information on new inventions, Siebert distinguishes two categories. One consists of government-supported research organizations and the other consists of private firms. With respect to inventions made by the first category, the mobility of knowledge is usually quite high, 'because government-supported research organizations normally tend to communicate their research results' (in general basic research results), whereas private firms try to conceal their information, in consideration of competition[14]. The hypothesis that could be deduced from this aspect is that the more government-supported research institutions in a region, the greater is the mobility of its knowledge.

The second factor highlighted by Siebert is the receiver of the information on new innovations. These receivers (presumably firms) must be able and willing to implement a new invention in their normal procedures. With respect to the ability to implement innovations, Richardson (1973) states that an indispensable factor for the spread of innovation in production techniques, processes and new managerial techniques 'to lagging regions is the presence of high calibre managers, scientists, technologists and centres of the decision-making in these areas' (Richardson, 1973, p. 123).

> Such potential adopters may be heavily concentrated in the core industrial regions of the economy (Ullman, 1958) and may also be relatively immobile, while the propensity for managers and technologists to be created domestically in the backward regions may be a function of the regions' past economic structure, social system and educational provision (Richardson, 1973, p. 123).

The importance of willingness is stressed by Siebert, as he argues that the greater the dissatisfaction with existing procedures in a region, the higher the willingness to adopt new methods. As Richardson (1973, p. 124) puts it: 'diffusion may be delayed if innovation requires new kinds of knowledge on the part of the adopter, new modes of behaviour or the coordinated efforts of different groups and organizations'. This argument was originally made by Mansfield (1968) and Day (1970). In addition to this argument, Siebert notes

---

[14] It should be noticed that knowledge generated by governmental institutions does not always have a high feasibility for private firms. Quite often private firms need different kinds of research (more applied research) than is offered by the governmental research institutions (merely basic research).

that new inventions arising from basic research done by government research institutions often need further research of private firms, which are unequally distributed over the regions. Therefore, 'the existing spatial structure, that is, the distribution of industry over space, determines the possible application of the new basic knowledge' (Siebert, 1969, p. 71). For example, if there is a large concentration of firms in a certain branch of industry in a certain region, it is obvious that inventions which are technically related to the techniques used in this branch will be adopted more than proportionally in this specific region. Another aspect of the same argument is that 'many innovations are applicable only to an individual industry, and in this case the presence of that industry in a region is obviously a necessary precondition for the innovation to be adopted in the area' (Richardson, 1973, p. 124).

Thirdly, the communication between sender and receiver has to be efficient. Siebert makes a distinction between formal and informal communication. This distinction 'affects the distribution of new basic knowledge'. Firms which have informal contacts with research institutes may receive more information flows. Siebert argues that 'the firms near the universities may be better and more quickly informed due to informal communication flows' (Siebert, 1969, p. 71). Thus, regions with many of those firms will have access to a higher amount of knowledge. Jaffe (1989) gives empirical evidence in support of this hypothesis. Based on an analysis of patent data he concludes that 'university research causes industry R&D and not vice versa. Thus a state that improves its university research system will increase local innovation both by attracting industrial R&D and augmenting its productivity' (Jaffe, 1989, p. 968).

Other factors that impede the mobility of knowledge in this respect are the transmission interval[15], the patent system[16], and factors such as the availability of financial means to innovate or imitate; profit requirements; and the size of the firms in the region[17].

Based on set theory, Siebert concludes that in equilibrium a specialization pattern will occur. Some regions will specialize in innovation, because they

---

[15] The time between the adoption of the innovation by one firm and the competitor of this firm knowing about it (Siebert, 1969). See also Friedman, J., *A General Theory of Polarised Development*, the Ford Foundation, Urban and regional advisory program in Chile, Santiago, Chile, 1967, p. 13.

[16] The patent system of a country has an influence on the whole country and not a specific influence on one certain region. However, a patent system can impede the mobility of knowledge and the scope for imitation.

[17] The size of the firms in a region has an influence on innovation and imitation. The presence of large firms can stimulate or impede innovation depending on different schools of thinking. Likewise, competition between firms is assumed to support or impede innovation (again depending on the view).

show the most favourable environment for innovating in their region, while others will specialize in imitation, or adoption. The degree of mobility of knowledge will have no influence on this distribution. Innovation will be polarized irrespective of the degree of mobility of knowledge, for the following reasons. First, if information on new technical knowledge is *immobile*, there exists a tendency for polarization, because the new technical knowledge will be held as secret as possible by the firm which made the invention. In addition, the patent system may prevent a wide spread of innovations. Therefore, only the spatial point where the invention occurred will use the new technical knowledge[18].

If, on the other hand, information on new technical knowledge is perfectly *mobile*, a partially or totally polarized incidence of new technical knowledge may also be expected, since not all spatial points will fulfil the necessary requirements for an innovation. There might be spatial points which have more favourable conditions for imitating than for the further development of a new invention; therefore these spatial points will not implement the new knowledge immediately, but wait for other regions to implement it. Thus, technical knowledge will be polarized in those regions which have the most favourable environment for innovation.

3.3 Economic geography

In recent years, a combination of the above two streams of literature has developed namely economic geography. Economic geography deals with questions such as how the spatial pattern of innovation comes about and to what extent innovations affect the growth (and decline) of regions. In addition, the rise and growth of clusters of firms is considered in this literature.

With respect to the former two issues, Boschma and van der Knaap (1997) try to explain the location of major innovations that generate new industries by applying the Windows of Locational Opportunity (WLO) concept (Boschma, 1994; Storper and Walker, 1989) to these topics. The WLO concept is a theoretical concept that considers issues such as indeterminacy, creativity and accidental events to be important in determining the spatial location of newly emerging industries. The first of these, spatial indeterminacy, points out that new industries might have other requirements

---

[18] One critical remark seems to be in place here. Siebert abstracts from the diffusion of an invention over space by multinational firms. It is obvious that a multinational firm will try to implement an invention originating from one of its plants, in all its geographically dispersed locations. Consequently, Siebert would observe less polarization if he included the efforts of multinational firms, even when immobile knowledge is considered.

as to location than existing industries. This results in new industries needing to locate in other geographical places than existing industries. The spatial structures and conditions that have emerged in a region, closely related to its individual history, will not necessarily provide favourable conditions for newly emerging industries. Therefore, these spatial practices will not predetermine the location of newly emerging industries. Second, creativity, or 'human agency', points to the fact that the specific requirements new industries have as to their location might only become clear as the industries develop. So when time passes, the specific needs of new industries become clear; therefore, new industries depend on their creative capacity to generate or attract their own favourable conditions in the region. Finally, accidental events ('randomness') indicates that regions might differ with respect to their ability to generate or attract new industries, due to their different individual histories. Regions differ in providing triggers or incentives for solutions to location-specific problems and for raising opportunities for industries. These triggers might be induced by small, arbitrary events that have happened in the past. Therefore, the location of new industries is highly uncertain and unpredictable. The flexibility needed to adapt the local environment to the developing requirements of the new industries may also differ across regions and change over time. These three points lead Boschma and van der Knaap to the conclusion that newly emerging industries are likely to develop independently of spatial structures and conditions laid out in the past and that the ability of regions to create new industries may change drastically as time passes.

The literature concerning the last issue, the clustering of firms, can roughly be divided into two strands: a stream that does not assume that technology or knowledge spillovers play an important role in the clustering of firms ~ especially high-tech firms ~ (Krugman, 1991; Rauch, 1993) and a stream that does assume that knowledge spillovers are the main reason behind the clustering of high technology firms (Audretsch and Feldman, 1996; Feldman and Florida, 1994).

In the first (a-spatial) view, knowledge spillovers take place as a result of long-term interactions between suppliers and manufacturers. The mutual trust, built in a number of years, allows suppliers and manufacturers to set up coordinated research programs for the development of new ideas. Mutual guest researchers intensify the spillover of knowledge from one firm to the other (Aoki, 1986). However, these networks are not established by geographic proximity. A long-term contact and a continuous exchange of information allow the development of expertise (Echeverri-Caroll and Hunnicutt, 1997). Thus, knowledge spillovers take place only if a firm establishes a trustful relationship with other firms. This is independent of location and spatial proximity. The reasons behind the observed clustering of high tech firms are the same as the reasons why firms in general tend to cluster, according to Krugman (1991).

In the literature reference is often made to the three Marshallian reasons for geographic localization, which are: (i) the presence of a pooled market of workers with specialized skills; (ii) the phenomenon that 'an industrial center allows the provision of nontraded inputs specific to an industry in a greater variety and at lower cost,' (Krugman, 1991, p. 37); (iii) technology spillovers might play a role, because information flows more easily over small distances (present within an industrial centre) than over larger distances. Krugman stresses that 'forces for localization other than those involving high technology are quite strong', (Krugman, 1991, p. 53). It is not the will to benefit from knowledge spillovers that drives agglomeration, but factors such as increasing returns to scale and transaction costs. In his thinking, geographic concentration will grow and persist, once established. Every manufacturer will choose one single location to serve the market, because of the existence of scale economies. In order to keep the transportation costs to a minimum, the manufacturer will choose a location with a large local demand. However, the local demand will be large precisely where the majority of manufacturers choose to locate. Thus, there is a circularity that tends to keep a cluster of firms in existence once it is established (Krugman, 1991, p. 15). With respect to the geographic location of a new cluster, Krugman argues that clusters may arise at any location, dependent on historical events.

Summarizing, this stream in economic geography does not attach great value to technology as a factor for firms to cluster together. The major contribution of this stream is the general awareness that transportation costs are important as a factor influencing the geographical concentration. In early papers by von Thünen (1826), Christaller (1933) and Lösch (1954), transportation costs were already taken into account as playing an important role; however, with the event of the neo-classical growth model, the factor of transportation was discarded, at least by economists. This new awareness of transportation costs leads to new attention for government investment on infrastructure. It has become clear that an efficient infrastructure is an essential condition for lasting economic growth.

Another body of literature, which also can be classified under the heading of economic geography, puts more emphasis on knowledge spillovers. In this literature, it is assumed that a low geographical distance facilitates knowledge spillovers between firms. Moreover, high technology firms agglomerate to access knowledge externalities, in contrast with non-high tech firms which agglomerate for reasons mentioned by Krugman, like scale economies and low transport costs. This idea is based on the assumption that communication is easier (informal) and more productive in places where skilled workers are geographically close together. Information flows more easily locally than over greater distances (Acs, FitzRoy and Smith, 1994). The flow of information leading to new products and processes takes place through a variety of channels, like conferences, trade shows, seminars, joint research projects and guest researchers. It is easier for an intellectual breakthrough to cross the hallway or the street than the country or the ocean (Echeverri-Caroll and Hunnicutt, 1997). Almeida and Kogut (1996) argue that the transport of ideas is only limited by the quality and availability of communication, which is likely to be higher locally. This argument is also embedded in the assumption that the flow of knowledge (particularly tacit knowledge (Storper, 1995; Morgan, 1997)) is geographically bounded (Marshall, 1920).

Accepting the idea that knowledge spillovers take place and that they are, to some extent, locally bounded[19], leads to certain expectations about the resulting distribution of knowledge across space. One would expect that over time a pattern of geographical agglomerations of innovative activities would occur. Empirically, several studies have been undertaken to investigate whether a spatial concentration of innovative activity is present. Some early contributions (Muiler and Nejedly, 1971; Buswell and Lewis, 1970) present empirical evidence of regional R&D concentration in European countries. The former study is carried out for Czechoslovakia, while the latter focuses on the United Kingdom. In another study, Malecki (1980) documented the location of R&D activities within the US. He concludes that industrial R&D is concentrated in large urban regions.

More recent research focused on evidence from output measures of innovative activity for the US. Several recent studies for the US (among others Jaffe, Traijtenberg and Henderson, 1993; Audretsch and Feldman, 1996; Feldman, 1994) examined the extent to which innovative as well as economic activity clusters spatially. Jaffe, Trajtenberg and Henderson (1993), Audretsch and Feldman (1996) and Feldman (1994a and b) observe differences in spatial concentration of innovative activity and economic activity both across regions and across branches of industry. Concerning em-pirical evidence of sectoral differences in spatial clustering (of innovativeness and production), Audretsch and Feldman (1994) find that 'the spatial concentration of innovative activity in particular industries is considerably greater than for all of manufacturing' (p. 12). Especially the computer industry and pharmaceuticals display a large geographic concentration. Breschi (1995), who examined patent data from the European Patent Office

---

[19] Meaning that locations nearby an innovative location will have a larger chance of receiving a knowledge spillover than locations far away.

over the period 1978-1991, finds evidence of 'quite large differences across sectors in the degree of spatial dispersion and asymmetries', (Breschi, 1995, p. 14). He notes that chemical-pharmaceutical and electrical-electronic sectors are characterized by high concentrations.

4. CONCLUDING REMARKS

This book fits in the line of research followed by economic geography. Since the central issue of this book is to broaden the understanding of knowledge spillovers (across space), the neo-classical line of thinking is discarded, because it considers knowledge to be completely mobile and spreading instantaneously to all geographical places. A more appropriate set of theories with regard to the central issue consists of the technology gap approach, which concentrates on diffusion over countries. However, technology gap theory tends to disregard the factor space. Technology is regarded as spreading to a country, because of the specific characteristics of that country, and geographic proximity does not play a role in this respect. The so-called spatial factors like agglomeration economies and growth poles as used by geographers are not addressed in this set of theories. Only the geographic stream of researchers used these concepts.

This book will try to fill this gap by introducing concepts from geography into a technology gap model, thereby effectively combining the two approaches. Knowledge spillovers are thought to be locally bounded and important for (local) economic development. The focus will be on regional knowledge spillovers, instead of spillovers on a country-level (as is generally adopted by technology gap models).

3. Evolutionary Thinking

The aim of this chapter is to introduce evolutionary thinking as an approach to explaining economic behaviour. Furthermore, this chapter will focus on the combination of evolutionary thinking with economic geography as discussed in Chapter 2. Figure 3.1 shows how the different sections are related.

Figure 3.1: Schematic overview of the sections

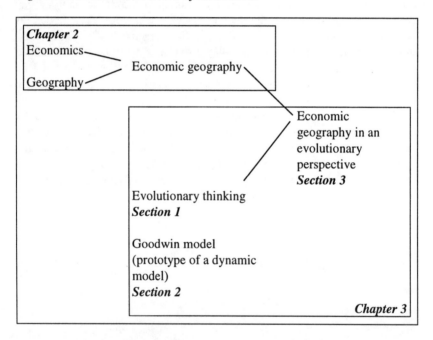

We will first look at the origins of evolutionary thinking. Via the various ideas and concepts and their applications to economic issues, we will direct attention to a prototype of a dynamic model of economic evolution, the Goodwin model. This model underlies the main model developed in the remainder of this book. Finally, Section 3 will give an overview of the work done in the field of economic geography from an evolutionary perspective.

1. AN INTRODUCTION TO EVOLUTIONARY THINKING

A central concept in evolutionary theory is bounded rationality (Simon, 1986). This is opposed to the traditional neo-classical assumption that agents are fully rational in taking decisions (rational expectations or full certainty)[20]. In neo-classical theory, this assumption is needed in order to be able to calculate a market equilibrium (by optimization). Evolutionary thinking argues instead that all agents are different (variation) and behave according to individual specific behaviour rules, which might not be fully rational but nevertheless are rational in some sense. Polanyi (1958) argued that human beings are unaware that their behaviours are based on partially opaque deliberations. The idea of bounded rationality has several implications, for one that agents do not have perfect knowledge about all possible events that might happen (uncertainties). Second, agents are not aware of the full consequences of every possible decision they can take at a certain moment (imperfect information). Firms pay attention to only a small part of their direct environment (they do not make a full model of the economy as assumed by neo-classical economists); therefore, they act under imperfect information and uncertainty. In a situation of strong uncertainty and imperfect information, firms cannot act fully rationally; instead, they use standardized rules, which, on average, lead to desirable outcomes. These rules may differ between individual firms (as explained above). Especially, innovation and technology are phenomena that are subject to imperfect information and uncertainty. The availability of information about a technology becomes progressively less imperfect through learning effects during the period of adoption and use of the technology itself (diffusion process) (Coombs, Saviotti and Walsh, 1987). However, even when the information exists, access to it is costly and varies widely among firms. The differential access to information and knowledge and the differential actions based upon this information are a few of the most important variables in determining a firm's success.

In this respect, it is important to stress the heterogeneity of agents (firms, species), which is also a central idea in evolutionary thinking. The different approaches among firms find their origin in the different circumstances in which firms function. The environment, past events, internal organization or even psychological factors, all leave a mark on a firm's behaviour rules

---

[20] In recent literature the differences between neo-classical theories and evolutionary theories have become smaller and blurred, since neo-classical models incorporate more and more imperfections, such as imperfect information (which could be viewed as an equivalent of bounded rationality) and heterogeneity of agents. Examples are Krugman (1996) and Sargent (1993).

(Dosi, 1988). Therefore, there is no such thing as a representative agent in economic reality (contrary to what is argued by neo-classical theory). All agents differ.

The outcome of the differential use of standardized rules will differ from the market equilibrium (under rational expectations and full certainty) as supposed by neo-classical economists. In traditional neo-classical thinking a market equilibrium is calculated by equalizing several factors, for instance supply and demand, at a certain moment. Evolutionary economists propose the selection mechanism as a substitute for the market equilibrium (Nelson and Winter). The differences across agents determine which are the fittest to survive in the market environment. Consequently, the equilibrium is no longer static, but dynamic instead. The growth of some firms and decline of others is a process that continues over time. This is described by a dynamic equilibrium. A dynamic equilibrium (or evolutionary equilibrium (Dosi et al., 1990)) defines a state in which there is still motion while the equilibrium in itself can be moving as well and in that sense be a moving target (Gomulka, 1990). According to Gomulka this movement of the equilibrium is fused by the process of innovation: 'The constant inflow of new ideas, changing fast the environment in which firms operate, makes each situation a new one, the past experience not always an asset, and the situation-specific optimal solution a moving target' (Gomulka, 1990, p. 70).

The question arises how to formulate an economic model along the lines of evolutionary thinking. Such an economic model can be set up by using a theoretical framework from biology, in which variety and change are the driving forces of growth.

In biology, evolutionary thinking started with Darwin's ideas about how life came about on this planet. In Darwin's view, species develop under pressure from the struggle for existence. There are three elements that together capture Darwin's theory. These are recombination, mutation and selection. Reproduction causes offspring to resemble their parents by inheritance. Reproduction takes place by a process of recombination, in which the genetic information of two parents is reshuffled and combined into a new genetic string for the offspring. When certain genetic information leads to characteristics that are favourable for survival, those individuals in a population that possess this information will tend to reproduce at a faster pace, simply because their higher survival rate enables them to live and reproduce longer (on average).

When left on its own, that is to say, without introducing new genetic information into a population, such a process of selection will thus lead to a population in which the 'favourable' genes dominate. Every now and then, however, random mistakes will be made during the copying of genetic information associated with the recombination process. Such random mutation may occasionally lead to new 'favourable' genes, thereby introducing new impulses to the selection process.

Consider the following example. To the north of the Amazon area, there is a river in which guppies live. In the upper course, the river is small and shallow. The water flows very fast and there are few predators. The male guppies are very colourful in this part of the river, in order to attract many female guppies. Thus, colourfulness is associated with a high reproduction rate, which leads to the selection of colourful males. In the lower course, the river is wide and deep, and many big fish ~ which like to eat little guppies ~ are present. The guppy males are unobtrusive in colour. The survival pressure in the lower course is against colourfulness, because bright colours are easily detected by predators. If a population of guppies moves from the upper course to the lower course, it is observed that with every generation the guppies get darker in colour.

Another view on the evolution of life was developed by a scientist named Lamarck in the beginning of the nineteenth century. The Lamarckian view is different from the Darwinian view in that Lamarck considers active learning. The individual learns from other individuals that a certain character is favourable for survival or producing offspring and hence adopts this characteristic. In biology, this Lamarckian view is discredited. A giraffe did not consciously lengthen his neck in order to reach the leaves at the high branches in the tree. The Darwinian view ~ that giraffes with genetic information for longer necks survived because they were able to access food ~ is much more adequate here. Biological evolution takes place by 'genetic' learning not 'individual' learning.

However, in economics the Lamarckian view seems much more appropriate. The Lamarckian view is applicable to firms and agents in that people (or groups of people) are able to *learn from experience* or from other people's experiences. Mutation can therefore be seen as endogenous instead of exogenous. People learn during their lifetime and not because of genetic selection.

The whole literature around learning curves (Stiglitz, 1987) takes up the idea of learning from experience. Experience in doing something enhances the efficiency with which it is done. Similarly, as a result of production, productivity increases (the Verdoorn effect, see also Chapter 2). Stiglitz (1987) labels this form of learning as learning-by-doing. He also distinguishes other forms of learning, like learning-by-using and learning-by-learning. The Verdoorn effect will be implemented in the model developed in the remainder of this book (see Chapter 4). Agglomeration economies and cumulative causation (Myrdal, 1957) as discussed in Chapter 2 are different concepts which are based on this same idea. They constitute the geographical counterparts of the economic concept of the Verdoorn law. Arthur (1990) applies the idea of increasing returns to the pattern of industry location. He takes the argument one step further by arguing that after a certain point in time a so-called lock-in effect occurs, meaning that a series of historical events (eventually) results in a certain spatial pattern of innovative (and economic) activity. An initial specialization of a region in a certain innovative activity is reinforced, and a lock-in process causes innovative activities to concentrate spatially. The locational pattern of innovative and economic activity is therefore path-dependent (and also dependent on the individual actions of the agents). This spatial view on evolutionary economics will be reviewed in more detail later in this chapter (Section 3.3).

To apply the Lamarckian view on the economy, we need to find economic counterparts to the biological concepts of mutation, replication and selection. Nelson and Winter (1982) note an analogy to the biological gene in established procedures, business strategies, policies and habits, described as 'routines'. 'These routines play the role that genes play in biological evolutionary theory' (Nelson and Winter, 1982, p. 14). Routines determine the possible behaviour of the firm. They are passed through during the time the firm exists and new-built plants often have the same routines. Routines are selectable in the sense that firms with better working (profit-generating) routines grow in market share. Nelson and Winter introduce the concept of 'search' which 'is the counterpart of that of mutation in biological evolutionary theory' (p. 18). Search involves the way routines change and improve over time. Economic selection happens through market competition. 'Market environments provide a definition of success for business firms, and that definition is very closely related to their ability to survive and grow' (p. 9). This is analogue to the idea of the survival of the fittest in natural selection. Firms that have adopted successful routines (through an effective search) will experience a growth in their market share, whereas other firms will lose in market share and might be forced to leave the market.

To put the concept of natural selection into mathematical terms use is often made of sets of difference or differential equations[21]. This approach will be adopted in Chapters 4, 5 and 6 of this book. The selection mechanism as described above can be captured in a simple equation, called the replicator equation (Fischer, 1930) (Equations (3.1) and (3.2)):

---

[21] Section 2 will give insight into one particular dynamic model.

$$\dot{X}_i = \alpha X_i (E_i - \overline{E}) \qquad (3.1)$$

$$\overline{E} = \sum_i^n E_i X_i, \qquad (3.2)$$

where X denotes the proportion of agent i in a population of n agents, E points to the competitiveness (fitness) of an agent and a bar indicates the average level of fitness of the population of n agents[22]. A dot above a variable points to the time derivative. This equation shows that the growth in proportion of a firm (the market share) is a function of the firm's competitiveness and the average competitiveness of all firms. Market shares change as a result of firm behaviour. In Section 2 we will come back to the formal modelling of evolutionary principles.

The replicator equation originates from biology in which species compete in the struggle for life. In biology, it is clear that the gene takes the role of fundamental unit of selection. In economics, the fundamental unit of selection is less clear. Similar to the growth and decline of firms is the growth and decline of technologies, which can be modelled using the same principle. Just as firms compete in the market environment (and species compete biologically), methods or technologies can compete for a market of adopters (Arthur, 1988). In fact, in economic literature the replicator equation is successfully applied to several units of selection (Silverberg, 1988).

2. FORMAL MODELLING

The replicator equation, as explained in the previous section, does not provide a detailed economic description of how economic selection takes place. It argues that above-average competitive firms grow more rapidly, but does not specify how exactly these growth rate differentials arise.

Silverberg (1984) proposed the Goodwin (1967) model as a prototype model of economic evolution. This model is a so-called predator-prey model (or Lotka-Volterra model), which has been shown to be formally equivalent to a replicator equation by Hofbauer and Sigmund (1988, pp. 134~5). In Silverberg's interpretation of the model, a common wage rate provides the selection mechanism, thereby giving selection explicit economic meaning. The rest of this section will explain the Goodwin model and Silverberg's interpretation of it.

---

[22] Note that in this simple context E_i is a constant.

Goodwin's model is in the line of the predator-prey equation system of Lotka (1956) and Volterra (1927) (see Gandolfo, 1996; Lorenz, 1989; Gabisch and Lorenz, 1989). Instead of the competing species of predators and preys, Goodwin models a society of capitalists and workers. The workers spend all their income wL on consumption, in which w denotes the real wage rate and L is employment. Capitalists save and invest all their income that is solely constituted of profits, determined by production Y minus labour costs wL. C denotes capital and a denotes labour productivity, which is defined as Y/L. Labour productivity is assumed to grow at a constant rate ϕ. N denotes labour supply, which is assumed to grow at a constant rate η.

Since investment, I, equals the growth of capital, which in turn equals savings, S, we have $I = S = Y - wL$, which can be rewritten as

$$\dot{C} = (1 - w/a)Y, \tag{3.3}$$

in which w/a is the wage income share in production and thus $(1- w/a)$ denotes the share of profits in production. The growth rate of the capital stock is then given by:

$$\dot{C}/C = \frac{(1 - w/a)Y}{C} = (1 - w/a)/\sigma, \tag{3.4}$$

in which σ $(= C/Y)$ denotes the capital-output ratio, which is assumed to be constant. This also implies

$$\dot{C}/C = \dot{Y}/Y. \tag{3.5}$$

Labour productivity is exogenously determined, therefore employment, L, is given by $L = Y/a$. Logarithmic differentiation gives

$$\dot{L}/L = \dot{Y}/Y - \phi = (1 - w/a)/\sigma - \phi. \tag{3.6}$$

The two central variables in the Goodwin model are the employment rate (L/N), hereafter denoted by v, and the wage income share in production: $w/a \equiv u$. Logarithmic differentiation of v gives

$$
\begin{aligned}
&\dot{v}/v = \dot{L}/L - \dot{N}/N \\
&\dot{v}/v = \dot{Y}/Y - \phi - \eta \\
&\dot{v}/v = (1 - w/a)/\sigma - (\phi + \eta) \\
&\dot{v}/v = -u/\sigma - (\phi + \eta) + 1/\sigma \Leftrightarrow \\
&\dot{v} = (-u/\sigma - (\phi + \eta) + 1/\sigma)v.
\end{aligned}
\tag{3.7}
$$

The same procedure for u leads to

$$\dot{u}/u = \dot{w}/w - \dot{a}/a$$
$$\dot{u}/u = \dot{w}/w - \phi. \tag{3.8}$$

Goodwin assumes that the wage rate follows a Phillips curve relation as displayed in Figure 3.2.

Figure 3.2: Phillips curve

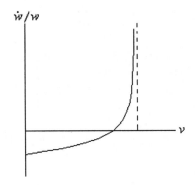

Taking a linear approximation to show the movements of v near the vertical line, we can write

$$\dot{w}/w = -\gamma + \rho v, \tag{3.9}$$

where γ and ρ are positive constants. Inserting this in the equation for the growth rate of u, this yields

$$\dot{u}/u = -\gamma + \rho v - \phi \Leftrightarrow$$
$$\dot{u} = (-(\phi + \gamma) + \rho v)u. \tag{3.10}$$

From Equations (3.7) and (3.10), we obtain the following system of equations:

$$\begin{cases} \dot{v} = (-u/\sigma - (\phi + \eta) + 1/\sigma)v \\ \dot{u} = (-(\phi + \gamma) + \rho v)u. \end{cases} \tag{3.11}$$

Such a system of equations is known as a predator-prey model (Lorenz, 1989). The employment rate v acts as the prey, while the wage bill share, u, serves as a predator.

Using the definitions

$$-(\phi + \eta) + 1/\sigma \equiv e, 1/\sigma \equiv f, (\phi + \eta) \equiv g, \rho \equiv h, \tag{3.12}$$

we can rewrite the system as

$$\begin{cases} \dot{v} = (e - fu)v \\ \dot{u} = (-g + hv)u. \end{cases} \tag{3.13}$$

The parameters f, g and h are positive by definition. It seems realistic to assume $1/\sigma > (\phi + \eta)$ (Gandolfo, 1996), so $e > 0$.

The equilibria of the system can be found when we set the time derivative of v and the time derivative of u both equal to zero. There appear to be two equilibrium points, namely $(v_1^*, u_1^*) = (0, 0)$ and $(v_2^*, u_2^*) = (g/h, e/f)$. To determine the characteristics of the equilibria the Jacobian is evaluated at each point:

$$Jacobian = \begin{pmatrix} e - fu & -fu \\ hu & -g + hv \end{pmatrix},$$

$$J(0,0) = \begin{pmatrix} e & 0 \\ 0 & -g \end{pmatrix}, \tag{3.14}$$

$$J(g/h, e/f) = \begin{pmatrix} 0 & -fg/h \\ he/f & 0 \end{pmatrix}.$$

In (v_1^*, u_1^*) the determinant and the trace of the Jacobian equal $-eg$, which is negative, indicating that the origin is a saddlepoint. It is clear that in (v_2^*, u_2^*) the determinant of the Jacobian equals eg, which is positive, and the trace of the Jacobian equals zero. This leads to the conclusion that (v_2^*, u_2^*) is the central point of a vortex. The system possesses closed orbits, instead of spirals[23]. The initial values of v and u determine which of the infinitely many closed orbits describes the actual behaviour of the system.

---

[23] See the Hirsch/Smale theorem in Lorenz (1989, p. 54; symbols have been changed in accordance with the notation used here): 'Every trajectory of the Lotka/Volterra equations is a closed orbit (except the equilibrium (v_2^*, u_2^*) and the co-ordinate axes).'

Figure 3.3: The Goodwin cycle

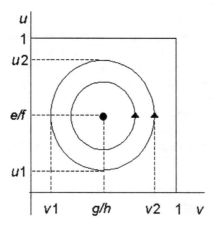

Figure 3.3 displays the system in motion. The x-axis shows the employment share *v*, which by the equation for the Phillips curve determines the rate of growth of the wage rate. The vertical axis shows the distribution of income. The workers' share is determined by the distance from the origin to the value of *u* and the capitalists' share is defined by 1 – *u*, which, multiplied by 1/σ gives the profit rate and the rate of output growth. Goodwin (1967) described the economic mechanism underlying the motion of an arbitrary point as follows:

> When profit is greatest, $u = u1$, employment is average, $v = g/h$ and the high growth rate pushes employment to its maximum *v2* which squeezes the profit rate to its average value *e/f*. The deceleration in growth lowers employment (relative) to its average value again, where profit and growth are again at their nadir *u2*. This low growth rate leads to a fall in output and employment to well below full employment, thus restoring profitability to its average value because productivity is now rising faster than wage rates ... The improved profitability carries the seed of its own destruction by engendering too a vigorous expansion of output and employment, thus destroying the reserve army of labour and strengthening labours bargaining power (pp. 168~9; symbols have been changed in accordance with the notation used here).

Silverberg (1984) elaborated on the Goodwin model, in order to describe selection in an environment with multiple firms. In the simplest form, his extension amounts to assuming there are two firms, each with a capital stock of their own. They hire labour on the same market, that is to say, they face the same wage rate, and economy-wide employment is equal to the sum of the two firms' labour demand. The firms are assumed to differ with regard to labour productivity, say $a_1 > a_2$ (and a_1 and a_2 are both constant). Thus, for all wage rates, the profit rate of firm 1 will be higher than that of firm 2, and hence firm 1 will grow more rapidly. In other words, firm 1 will increase its market share and drive firm 2 out of the market. Hence the model will converge to a special case of the above model, where $a = a_1$ and $\phi = 0$. More interesting dynamics may be obtained when the growth rates of labour productivity are endogenized (for example, the Silverberg, 1984 model in its full form). Chapter 6 of this model will propose such an endogenization for the case of a multi-country/multi-region economy. The next section will explain some of the general lines along which this will be done.

3. ECONOMIC GEOGRAPHY IN AN EVOLUTIONARY PERSPECTIVE

Allen and Sanglier (1978, 1979a, 1979b, 1981a and 1981b) developed one of the first evolutionary models in economics that pays attention to spatial effects. They designed a spatial model with respect to population dynamics and assume a mutual interaction between the change in the distribution of the population of a region and the employment pattern. The result is a dynamic model of interacting urban centres in which 'historical chance', that is, the fluctuations of the system, plays a vital role.

Arthur (1990) implements technology in a similar model of economic geography. He argues that a series of historical events (eventually) results in a certain spatial pattern of innovative (and economic) activity. An initial specialization of a region in a certain innovative activity is reinforced, and a lock-in process causes innovative activities to concentrate spatially. The locational pattern of innovative activity is therefore path-dependent.

In general, it can be said that increasing returns to location (economies of scale and agglomeration economies) and cumulative causation are the main ideas behind an evolutionary approach to economic geography. The existence of economies of scale stimulates a firm to locate in one geographical location instead of several dispersed plants. In addition, agglomeration economies induce innovative activities to cluster geographically. Agglomeration economies (see Chapter 2) imply that positive externalities will occur when economic (as well as innovative) activity is located in a geographically close area. A spatial concentration of economic activity and people generates positive effects on productivity, because, for instance, the opportunity for communication of ideas and experience becomes much larger than in case of the absence of such concentration. Furthermore, differences in innovativeness across regions may be persistent rather than transitory. This argument is based on Myrdal's (1957) theory of circular and cumulative causation (see Chapter 2, Section 2). The regional interpretation of this theory is that a region which starts with an economic or innovative advantage (for any reason), will go on to stay economically and innovatively ahead of other regions in the area under consideration. Since these differences in innovativeness will be persistent over time, a spatial pattern will occur that is characterized by spatial concentrations of innovation in certain regions.

Acknowledging the existence of localized knowledge spillovers may give a more realistic view on the resulting spatial pattern. Since knowledge will diffuse gradually to a bounded space, regions with a high proximity to an innovative (or economically strong) location will receive many spillovers and therefore have only small gaps towards the innovative region. The gaps will become larger at larger distances from the innovative location.

How could a regional spillover model be set up along these lines? It is realistic to assume that regions differ in characteristics and therefore are heterogeneous with respect to their behaviour. The specific characteristics of a region determine the amount of spillovers a region receives at a specific time and the potential for transmitting spillovers to other regions. Factors such as the educational system, the quality of the infrastructure and the state of technology set the extent to which a region can implement external knowledge. Regions differ with respect to such factors.

Furthermore, such a regional spillover system would be characterized by a continuous flow of spillovers from each region to other regions. At each period, there is interaction. The amount of spillovers that is received by a certain region depends on the past interactions within the whole system. The system is constantly in motion. Groups of regions grow, while others decline. Therefore, the process cannot be described in a static way (using the concept of market-equilibrium).

Evolutionary modelling is very apt to analyse such a multi-regional model. The different behaviours of regions with respect to receiving knowledge spillovers form the input to the selection mechanism. The selection mechanism explains the motion in the system. During the transitory dynamics regions with favourable characteristics at a certain moment will grow, but may decline after a while when other regions' favourable characteristics for growth emerge. In the end this system might lead to a dynamic equilibrium in which regions still grow (in terms of their knowledge stock) but have reached a stable (relative) position towards all other regions (if they are not falling behind instead, see Chapter 4). The dynamic character of such a regional spillover system is grasped by evolutionary modelling in the application of the selection mechanism.

The Goodwin-type model in this book will use the idea of localized knowledge spillovers to endogenize technology (labour productivity) in a regional context. In the model, the growth of labour productivity is set proportional to the growth in the knowledge stock. This growth rate, in turn, is determined by several factors (for details refer to Chapter 6), among others the spillovers received from all other regions in the world. The effect of increasing returns to location is present in the model in two forms. First, via the Verdoorn effect (agglomeration economies): productivity growth in a region is positively related to output growth in the same region. The second effect stems from geographical distance in combination with technological distance (as used in the technology gap models, see Chapter 2). The smaller the distance (geographical and/or technological) from an innovative region, the larger the amount of received spillovers and therefore the higher the growth rate of the knowledge stock of a region, which implies a higher growth rate of labour productivity.

Instead of a countrywide wage rate (as in Silverberg, 1984) the proposed model will use regionally determined wage rates. This implies that each region has its own Goodwin-cycle. Since the regions influence each other by means of spillovers in each time period, the vortexes (one for every region) are dependent on each other. In fact, centres move over time.

Chapter 4 will develop a system by which spillovers take place between regions. In Chapter 6, a Goodwin-type model, including such a spillover system, will be set up.

4. Introducing Geographical Distance in the Modelling of Technology Spillovers

The aim of this chapter is to integrate space as explained in Chapter 2 into technology gap models. The absence of space as an explaining factor in technology gap models is addressed in this chapter by extending a simple technology gap model with the concept of geographical distance. In order to do so this chapter is organized as follows. In Section 1, a spillover system is described. A region gets a certain amount of spillovers from its neighbour according to certain rules. These spillovers are the input to the growth of a region. In Section 2, the model is extended to a multi-region model. Section 3 outlines some general conclusions of the model.

1. DESCRIPTION OF THE MODEL

The model that is presented in this section will aim to incorporate several considerations from economic theory and geographic theory. As in other (empirical) catching up literature, the assumption will be adopted that technology is the only factor that influences output. In fact, output growth is a linear function of the growth of the knowledge stock.

$$\frac{\dot{Q}_i}{Q_i} = \beta \frac{\dot{K}_i}{K_i}, \tag{4.1}$$

in which Q_i denotes the level of output of region i and K_i points to the level of the knowledge stock of region i. β is a parameter. Dots above variables denote time derivatives.

Next, the equation of the knowledge stock in region i (K_i) is specified. The growth of the knowledge stock in region i is assumed to be a function of output growth (via the Verdoorn effect, see Chapter 2), spillovers received from surrounding (not necessarily contingent) regions (S_i), as well as an exogenous rate of growth (ρ_i).

$$\frac{\dot{K}_i}{K_i} = \alpha \, (\lambda \, \frac{\dot{Q}_i}{Q_i} + S_i + \rho_i), \tag{4.2}$$

in which α and λ are parameters.

The growth of the knowledge stock of a region is partly determined by the spillovers received from surrounding regions. For the explanation of the spillover term, it is convenient to first consider two regions; later on (Section 3) this framework will be extended and a multi-region model will be constructed. In the two-region setting it is assumed that there is one technologically advanced region and one backward region. There are two factors which determine spillovers between regions. The first is the existence of a technology gap, which induces spillovers from the advanced region to the backward region. This is the 'ordinary' way of modelling this, theoretically justified by the technology gap literature and analogous to the procedure developed by Verspagen (1991, 1992b). The second factor is geographical distance. A small geographical distance facilitates knowledge spillovers between regions. This assumption comes forward from geographical literature. The occurrence of face-to-face interaction between firms will be less intensive as the geographical distance between them is increased.

The modelling of the spillovers takes the following form:

$$S_i = \frac{\delta_i}{\gamma_{ij}} \, e^{-(\frac{1}{\delta_i} G_{ij} - \mu_i)^2}, \tag{4.3}$$

$$G_{ij} = \ln \frac{K_i}{K_j}, \tag{4.4}$$

in which S_i denotes the spillovers generated by region j and received by region i[24]. G_{ij} points to the technology gap of region i towards region j. Equation (4.4) gives the exact specification of the technology gap. γ_{ij} is the geographical distance between the two regions. If γ_{ij} increases, the spillover is reduced. δ_i points to the intrinsic learning capability of region i. The assumption, taken from technology gap models, is that regions which have a high capability to learn (because they have an educated workforce, good

---

[24] Note that the lower the initial stock of knowledge a region is endowed with, the more spillovers it will receive. This is similar to the concept of β-convergence (Barro, 1984; Baumol, 1986; De Long, 1988; Barro and Sala-i-Martin, 1991, 1992a, 1992b) in which a backward economy (an economy with a low initial level of GDP per capita) will grow faster than a rich economy and therefore catch up.

educational facilities, and/or a developed knowledge infrastructure) can implement the knowledge from other regions more easily. The part of the received knowledge that is valuable for these regions (in the sense that they can implement it straightaway) is much larger than for regions that have a low 'learning capability'. In Equation (4.3), a high learning capability assures that a region will receive many spillovers. μ_i can be interpreted as a catching up parameter, it determines the magnitude of the gap at which catch-up occurs. We will come back on this factor later. The technology gap (G_{ij}) is also used as an indicator of technological distance. G_{ij} is defined as the log of the ratio of the knowledge stocks of two regions.

The specific feature of introducing geographic distance in the way it is done in this model, is that there will always be spillovers (although they might be small) from one region to another. This is due to the measurement of geographic distance[25], which is always larger than, or equal to, one. Therefore, the spillover function is never exactly equal to zero (although it approaches zero in the limit). This is in contrast with other catch-up literature in which no spillovers exist if the knowledge stocks in the regions are equal. Thus, the model allows spillovers to occur in two directions, from the technological leader to backward region(s), and vice versa. Generally, the first stream will be largest, since the backward region can learn more than the advanced region. However, spillovers from a backward region to the leader region also take place because it could well be possible that the backward region has (developed) complementary knowledge, knowledge that was not yet in the hands of the leader. So there always is a small flow of knowledge from laggard to leader, although this quantity approaches zero for large gaps.

Figure 4.1: Spillover function of two regions

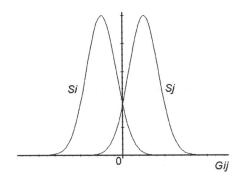

[25] Section 2 in Chapter 6 explains in detail how the geographic distance is measured.

If the spillover functions of two regions are drawn, (all parameters are assumed to be equal between the regions), we get Figure 4.1. As can be seen, the expression for the knowledge spillovers takes the shape of a Bell-function. Left from the vertical axis region j is the most advanced region, here region i receives the most spillovers. Right from the vertical axis the opposite is the case, that is, region i is the leader region. As can be seen in the figure, below the curve indicating the spillover j receives from i (S_j) there lies still a small part of the S_i line, indicating that, although region i is the leader, spillovers from region j to region i still take place, although they are small (see above). Another point that has to be noted is that the *net* spillover will be equal to zero in the case where the gap between the two regions is zero (that is, they have equal knowledge stocks). This emphasizes the unique working of this model. In this situation there are still spillovers (although the knowledge stream from region i to j is as large as the other way around), contrary to regular catch-up models, where knowledge spillovers are reduced to zero if knowledge stocks are equal between regions. The latter situation only holds, however, when parameters (ρ, λ, μ, δ) are equal between the two regions.

Figure 4.2 and Figure 4.3: Spillovers received by one region

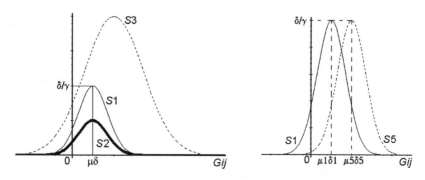

In Figure 4.2 the spillovers received by one region for a two-region model are displayed. With the help of this graph, many characteristics of the spillover function become clear. Note that the top of each spillover curve lies at a technology gap equal to $\mu_j\delta_j$. The maximal spillover corresponding to this is equal to δ_j/γ_{ij}. We take $S1$ as the starting point, and we consider what happens to the spillover function under certain conditions. First, an enlargement of the geographical distance between two regions will lead to lower spillovers received by each region, depicted by the thick line ($S2$, which shows the situation for the laggard region only). With the same technology gap, fewer spillovers occur. Second, an increase in the learning capability of the lagging region (δ_j) will cause the spillover function to behave as displayed by the dotted line (S3). The spillovers that region j will receive are now larger. The gap at which maximal spillovers occur is also larger, indicating that not only more spillovers are received, but also that the range over which spillovers increase as a function of the technology gap is larger. Thus, the laggard is able to learn more (magnitude of the spillover function) and more easily or earlier (at a larger technological distance). The top of the curve (which is equal to δ_j/γ_{ij}) has been replaced upward and to the right of the original position[26].

A third characteristic of the expression for the spillover can be shown with the help of Figure 4.3. If μ_j is increased, all other things being equal, the curve will shift to the right (S5). This has several effects. First, the level of spillovers in the case of equal knowledge stocks across regions ($G=0$), is smaller. This indicates that for relatively large μ, the model resembles a regular catch-up model, which is characterized by zero spillovers for zero technological distance.

Second, because the top of the curve moves to the right, catch-up becomes easier. At a larger technological distance, it is still possible to receive many knowledge spillovers, and, therefore, to catch up. The specifics of this mechanism will become clearer after we discuss the net spillover function.

2. THE DYNAMICS OF THE MODEL

To analyse the dynamics of this model, we take the time derivative of the technology gap in Equation (4.4) and substitute Equations (4.1), (4.2) and (4.3). For a two-region model this boils down to:

$$\dot{G}_{ij} = \frac{d}{dt} \ln \frac{K_i}{K_j} = \frac{\dot{K}_i}{K_i} - \frac{\dot{K}_j}{K_j} = \frac{\alpha}{1-\alpha\beta\lambda}((\rho_i - \rho_j) - (S_j - S_i)), \text{ with } 0 < \alpha\beta\lambda < 1 \tag{4.5}$$

in which α, β and λ are assumed to have the same value in each region. This expression can be analysed using Figure 4.4.

Two cases can be distinguished, one in which region i is the most advanced, and one in which region j is the leader region. Since the two cases are mirror images of each other, we will restrict ourselves to describing only

---

[26] To achieve this reaction of the spillover curve, the learning capability had to appear in two places in the spillover function (Equation 4.3).

one case, namely the one in which region i is the leader. In Figure 4.4, $S_j - S_i$ represents the difference in spillovers generated by the lagging and the leading region (the net knowledge spillover curve). This curve results from subtracting S_i from S_j[27]. $\rho_i - \rho_j$ displays the difference in the exogenous rate of growth of the knowledge stock between the two regions. If we assume that region i is the most advanced, it is expected that the exogenous rate of growth of the knowledge stock in region i exceeds that of region j, thus $\rho_i > \rho_j$ and therefore $\rho_i - \rho_j > 0$ (as drawn in the figure)[28]. The intersection points of the two curves correspond to equilibrium points (where the time derivative of the technology gap is equal to zero). The nature of these equilibrium points differs. The intersection point at which the S-curve has a positive slope is stable, whereas the other intersection point is unstable. Therefore, the arrows of motion can be drawn as is done in Figure 4.4. When the $S_j - S_i$ curve is below (above) the $\rho_i - \rho_j$ line, that means that the knowledge spillovers received by region j are smaller (larger) than the exogenous increase of the gap, resulting in a net increase (decrease) of the technology gap. Therefore, depending on the net knowledge spillovers, the technology gap either converges to the equilibrium point close to the vertical axis, or goes to infinity.

Figure 4.4: Net knowledge spillover curve

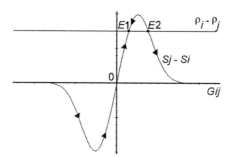

The position of the intersection points differs if one of the two curves, either $\rho_i - \rho_j$ or $S_j - S_i$, or both, move. In order to distinguish between the different effects we will first consider a variation in the difference in the exogenous rate of growth of the knowledge stock between the two regions, ρ_i

---

[27] Note that a net spillover curve doesn't necessarily intersect with the origin. In Figure 5.4 the learning capabilities δ_i and δ_j are assumed equal to each other, as well as the catch-up parameters μ_i and μ_j.

[28] As ρ_j exceeds ρ_i the intersection of the curve with the horizontal line is located at the left-hand side of the vertical axis. Here region j is the leader, therefore this assumption holds again.

$- \rho_j$. If the difference is enlarged in favour of the leader, the $\rho_i - \rho_j$ line in Figure 4.4 moves upward, meaning that the range of technology gaps at which catch-up occurs becomes smaller. Eventually, when the $\rho_i - \rho_j$ line shifts to a position above the net spillover curve, there will be no opportunities for catch-up. If, on the other hand, the exogenous rate of growth of the knowledge stock in the backward region is increased (for example, by expanding research efforts) up to a level comparable with the advanced region, that is, the $\rho_i - \rho_j$ line is positioned on the horizontal axis, the technology gap will eventually close and the regions will converge completely.

The second way of altering the position of the intersection points is to change the position of the spillover function $Sj - Si$, by varying the parameters γ, δ and/or μ. First, we consider a variation in the geographical distance between two regions. Of course this experiment seems a little odd, since we consider only two regions, and we cannot pick up one region and locate it somewhere else in order to decrease the geographical distance. However, this experiment is carried out in order to show the influence on the net spillover curve of this parameter. A decrease in the geographical distance has the effect that the spillover curves S_i and S_j increase proportionally to the decrease in geographical distance (explained by Figure 4.2) and the maximum of the $S_j - S_i$ curve in Figure 4.5 moves upwards[29].

Figure 4.5 (left): The impact of geographical distance
Figure 4.6 (right): Bifurcation diagram

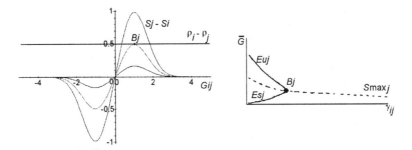

The bifurcation diagram is displayed in Figure 4.6[30]. The horizontal axis of the bifurcation diagram shows the values of the geographical distance parameter γ_{ij}. The vertical axis shows the equilibrium values of the

---

[29] The maximum also moves a little bit away from the y-axis, but this is a very small effect.
[30] Note that the figure should show a discontinuous graph (in the model a geographical distance is either 1 or 2, not 1.5); however, for visual reasons the individual points are connected.

technology gap. The line E_{sj} shows a stable equilibrium, while the line E_{uj} points to an unstable equilibrium. The line S_{maxj} represents the top of the net spillover curve in Figure 4.5. This figure shows that for high values of γ_{ij} no equilibrium value of the technology gap exists. If we look at the horizontal line $(\rho_i - \rho_j)$ in Figure 4.5, it becomes clear that there are positions of the net spillover curve, for which there is no intersection point with this line. For the threshold value of γ_{ij}, one equilibrium appears. This equilibrium point B_j is the point of tangency between the $\rho_i - \rho_j$ line and the $S_j - S_i$ curve. For values of γ_{ij} smaller than the threshold level, two equilibria exist, as described by the curves in the bifurcation diagram. As shown in Figure 4.6 the value of the stable equilibrium is always closer to zero than the maximum of the knowledge spillover term.

However, the geographical distance is not something that can be influenced by a region. What can be influenced is the intrinsic learning capability of a region. This is the second parameter that can move the $S_j - S_i$ curve. The effect of an increase in the learning capability of region j (δ_j) on the $S_j - S_i$ curve is displayed in Figure 4.7. Note that δ_i has not changed. It can clearly be seen that on the right-hand side of the figure the top of the curve has moved to the upper right of the figure and the curve does not intersect with the origin any more. What has happened on the left-hand side is a bit more difficult to see. The minimum point has moved upwards so that it is closer to the horizontal axis. Also, there is a small movement of the minimum point away from the vertical axis.

Figure 4.7 (left): The impact of the learning capability
Figure 4.8 (right): Bifurcation diagram

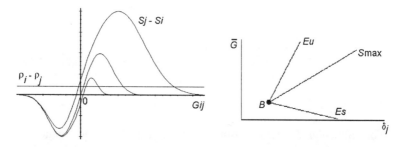

The bifurcation diagram now looks as displayed in Figure 4.8. On the horizontal axis, the learning capability is displayed. This figure shows that as the learning capability of the lagging region increases, a threshold level is reached at which the curves $S_j - S_i$ and $\rho_i - \rho_j$ in Figure 4.4 are tangent. This is the bifurcation point B. A further increase of the learning capability leads to two equilibria, a stable and an unstable one. Note that the E_s line for the stable equilibrium can even go below the horizontal axis if the difference in exogenous growth rates of the knowledge stock is small enough. This situation indicates a takeover in leadership by the (initially) lagging region. In Figure 4.7 the horizontal line $(\rho_i - \rho_j)$ intersects with the $S_j - S_i$ curve left from the vertical axis, where the gap is smaller than zero, indicating that region j is the leader region. The combination of a large learning capability in the lagging region together with a small difference in the exogenous rate of growth between laggard and leader gives rise to takeover. The backward region takes over the lead position.

Figure 4.9: The impact of the catch-up parameter on the spillover curve

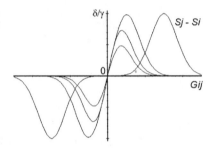

The final parameter that can be changed and will have an effect on the graph in Figure 4.4 is the catch-up parameter μ. We will increase μ_j and μ_i simultaneously $(\mu_i = \mu_j)$[31]. The effect on the net spillover curve $(S_j - S_i)$ is that the extrema will move away from the horizontal axis and the vertical axis, as displayed in Figure 4.9. As can be seen on the right-hand side of Figure 4.3, as μ goes to infinity, the top of the spillover curve (S_j) will go to δ/γ. As the catch-up parameter μ will increase in value, the net spillover function will approach the shape given by Equation (4.3). Therefore, the top of the net spillover curve $(S_j - S_i)$ will approach the value δ/γ. In the left-hand side of Figure 4.9 the minimum point will approach the value $-\delta/\gamma$ for the same reason.

---

[31] This assumption has the consequence that both regions are affected in the same manner by a variation in this parameter. Furthermore, the net spillover curve is forced to intersect with the horizontal axis by this assumption.

Figure 4.10: The impact of the catch-up parameter in more detail

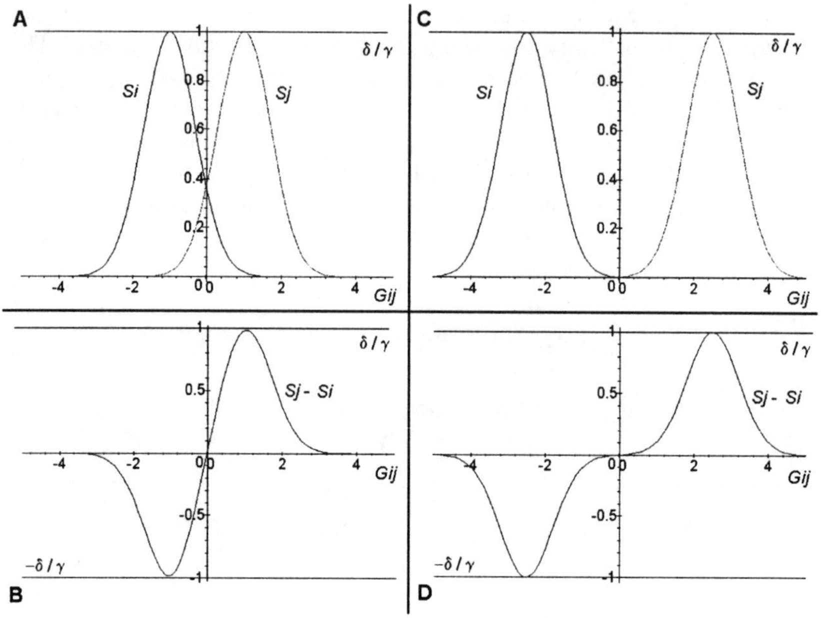

This is explained in Figure 4.10. The upper part (panels A and C) shows the individual spillover curves for each region, whereas the lower part (panels B and D) shows the net spillover curve. The left-hand side (panels A and B) points to a situation with a small μ, whereas the right-hand side (panels C and D) point to the case of a large μ. Note that in the case of a small catch-up parameter, the extrema of the net spillover curve (panel B) are below δ/γ (right-hand side) and above $-\delta/\gamma$ (left-hand side). In panel D the difference between the curve and the lines δ/γ and $-\delta/\gamma$ is negligibly small. This has the important consequence that an increase in μ will enlarge the effect of the geographic distance parameter in the model. A variation in the geographical distance will affect the figure in the following way. An increase (decrease) in γ will decrease (increase) the top of the net spillover curve proportionally if the catch-up parameter is large. Suppose μ is small (panels A and B), in this case a variation in γ (all other thing equal) will have a *less than proportional* effect. S_i becomes larger in terms of panel A, but S_j becomes larger as well, thus the top of $S_j - S_i$ will be lower than δ/γ[32].

---

[32] Figure 4.10 is based on numerical analysis.

Figure 4.11: Bifurcation diagram

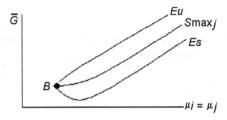

The bifurcation diagram now shows μ_i ($=\mu_j$) on the horizontal axis. As can be seen in Figure 4.11, the stable equilibrium first moves towards the vertical axis as μ_i ($=\mu_j$) is increased. If μ is increased even further, the stable equilibrium starts to move away from the y-axis with a steady pace. The reason for this can be seen in Figure 4.9. Here it is shown that the S_{max} curve approaches the value δ/γ (because the larger μ becomes, the more the S_i and S_j curve resembles a Bell-function), this implies that a further increase of μ leads to only a minimal increase in height of the curve, meaning that the E_s, E_u and S_{max} curves increase with a steady pace in the bifurcation diagram.

3. MULTI-REGION VERSION OF THE MODEL

Suppose we have a world with k regions, so that each region can be characterized by $k-1$ technology gaps (we omit the trivial case of G_{ii}). Spillovers are received from each of the other regions, so that the S terms in Equation (4.2) now become sums of spillovers over $k-1$ regions. This gives rise to the following modified form of Equation (4.5):

$$\dot{G}_{ij} = \frac{d}{dt} \ln \frac{K_i}{K_j} = \frac{\dot{K}_i}{K_i} - \frac{\dot{K}_j}{K_j} = \frac{\alpha}{1-\alpha\beta\lambda} \left((\rho_i - \rho_j) + (\Sigma_n S_{in} - \Sigma_n S_{jn}) - (S_j - S_i) \right),$$
$$\text{with } 0 < \alpha\beta\lambda < 1, \tag{4.5'}$$

in which $\Sigma_n S_{in}$ and $\Sigma_n S_{jn}$ denote the spillovers received by region i and j respectively from all regions n for which $n \neq i, j$ (this term is thus invariant to G_{ij}). Note that Equation (4.5') specifies the (growth of the) gap between the two regions i and j only. There are k regions in total, thus every region i has $k-1$ of these equations.

The right-hand side of Equation (4.5') consists of several important terms. The first and the second term between the large brackets, $(\rho_i - \rho_j)$ and $(\Sigma_n S_{in} -$

$\Sigma_n S_{jn}$), together, determine the position of the horizontal line in Figure 4.4[33]. Therefore, a movement in the horizontal line (and therefore in the horizontal position of $E2$) can be caused by two factors. First, a variation in the difference between the exogenous rates of growth of the knowledge stocks of two regions. Second, a difference across regions in the spillovers received from all other regions. For this term, the geographic location of a region is important. The third term in Equation (4.5'), $(S_j - S_i)$, determines the shape of the curve in Figure 4.4.

Figure 4.12: Example of a lattice

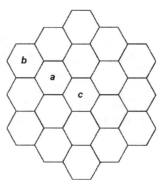

A brief example can illustrate this. Suppose there are two regions (*a* and *b*) in a lattice of *n* regions of which one (region *a*) has a central position in the lattice and the other (region *b*) is located at the border of the lattice. Figure 4.12 gives an illustration of this geographic situation for a lattice with 19 regions. Suppose the most advanced region (*c*) is located at the centre of the lattice and therefore is geographically close to region *a* ($\gamma_{ac} = 1$) and geographically distant ($\gamma_{bc} = 2$) from region *b*. We assume that the geographic location is the only parameter that differs across regions *a* and *b*. In all other respects regions *a* and *b* are completely the same. Now we examine the growth of the technological gap of each region towards the advanced region by using Equation (4.5'):

$$\dot{G}_{ac} = \frac{\alpha}{1-\alpha\beta\lambda}((\rho_c - \rho_a) + (\sum_n S_{cn} - \sum_n S_{an}) - (S_a - S_c))$$

$$\dot{G}_{bc} = \frac{\alpha}{1-\alpha\beta\lambda}((\rho_c - \rho_b) + (\sum_n S_{cn} - \sum_n S_{bn}) - (S_b - S_c))$$

---

[33] This is the case because both terms are exogenous to the net spillover function of the two regions under consideration. Note that $(\Sigma_n S_{in} - \Sigma_n S_{jn})$ denotes the spillovers that are received from all regions except the two for which the gap is determined.

Figure 4.13: The situation for region a and b respectively

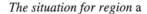 *The situation for region* a
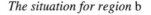 *The situation for region* b

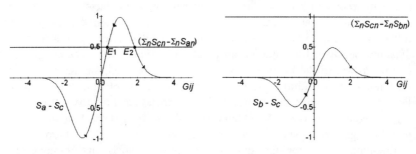

The difference in the gap between the two regions is determined by two terms. First, $(S_a - S_c)$ differs from $(S_b - S_c)$ as illustrated by the curves in Figure 4.13. Since region *a* is located closer to the most advanced region it will receive more spillovers from region *c* than region *b*.

The horizontal line in Figure 4.13 illustrates the second effect. Since region *a* is closer to all other regions, due to its central position, it will receive more spillovers from all other regions in the lattice, compared to region *b*. In other words, $\Sigma_n S_{an} > \Sigma_n S_{bn}$, indicating that $(\Sigma_n S_{cn} - \Sigma_n S_{an}) < (\Sigma_n S_{cn} - \Sigma_n S_{bn})$. The horizontal line will be lower for region *a*. It becomes clear that whereas region *a* has many possibilities to catch up and tend to the stable equilibrium point $E1$, region *b* may fall behind.

4. GENERAL CONCLUSIONS

In this chapter technological spillovers are assumed to be generated via two different factors, which are based on two different concepts of distance. First, geographical distance relative to another region is an important factor which determines the amount of knowledge spillovers. In addition, technological distance, that is, the technology gap, plays an important role. This refers to the degree to which a region is able to assimilate knowledge from other regions, and is measured by the level of the knowledge stock of one region relative to the level of the knowledge stock of another region. Related to this concept of technological distance is the learning capability (δ), which denotes the *intrinsic* capability of a region to implement knowledge from other regions. This concept differs from the technology gap in that the learning capability is a characteristic of a region, whereas the technology gap can differ (and can be measured at) several moments in time.

The difference in received spillovers between regions is an important determinant of the size of the equilibrium gap a region has with respect to another region. From the equation for the two-regional model (Equation (4.5)) it becomes clear that there is another important factor, namely, the differences in exogenous rates of the growth of the knowledge stock (ρ) can influence the gap to which a region tends to stabilize after the transitionary dynamics are over (the equilibrium point $E1$ in Figure 4.4). The exogenous rate of growth of the knowledge stock can be influenced, among others, by the amount of expenditures devoted to research and development in a region. For a backward region to increase the R&D expenditures relative to the other region, would lead to a shift in the horizontal line of Figure 4.4 and therefore to a lower gap with respect to the leader region; that is to say, catch-up.

Equation (4.5') for the multi-region model shows that besides the difference in exogenous rates of growth of the knowledge stock, there is another term, which has an influence on the height of the horizontal line and therefore the size of the equilibrium gap. This term is the difference in spillovers each region receives from all other regions except from the regions under consideration. Of course the learning capability of each region in the plane has an influence on these spillovers.

In short, it is concluded that space has an influence on catching up and falling behind. It becomes clear that since spillovers are assumed to be bilateral, many interactions across regions occur in each period of time. This makes the model too complex to analyse mathematically. Using simulations enables us to analyse the model in more detail. Chapter 5 will be devoted to this exercise.

Furthermore, from the set-up of the model it is clear that spillovers take the crucial role in the model. These spillovers take place according to several intuitive rules, such as (i) the shorter the distance between two places, the more spillovers will be transferred, and (ii) the higher the capability of a region to implement new technology, the more spillovers will be accommodated. These simple rules give occasion to an analysis by simulations for several regions on a plane. These simulations will be described in Chapter 5.

5. Simulation Results

Chapter 4 modelled technology spillovers across regions while taking into account geographic proximity and technological distance. This chapter will analyse the model by use of simulations.

Because spillovers are bilateral, the model in Chapter 4 describes many interactions between regions in each period of time. The non-linearity of the model potentially leads to a high sensitivity to the initial conditions or parameter constellations. However, by carrying out many simulations (with randomized initial conditions or parameter constellations) it is possible to examine the general behaviour of the model. In fact, when we look at the general behaviour, we find that certain patterns in the gaps of the knowledge stocks appear repeatedly.

The chapter is organised into six sections. The first explains the geographical spheres that are used for the simulations. Section 2 focuses on the measurement of geographical distance in the model. Several alternative ways of measuring and modelling geographical distance will be discussed. Next, results will be presented for several experiments in which the initial conditions and parameters are varied, starting in Section 3 with variations in the initial level of the knowledge stock. This is followed by two sections describing variations in parameters. Section 4 examines the effect of the learning capability, whereas Section 5 focuses on the influence of the exogenous rate of growth of the knowledge stock. Section 6 presents a summary and a conclusion.

1. DESCRIPTION OF THE ARTIFICIAL DATA AND THE ARTIFICIAL GEOGRAPHICAL SPHERES

The model described in the last chapter is analysed, generating artificial data and using artificial geographical spheres. Although the model in Chapter 4 fully describes interactions between regions, it does not provide a description of how regions are located in space. This section explains three different ways in which this gap will be filled. The three possible spatial structures considered are a lattice of honeycombs, a column and a globe. The first of these spheres is two-dimensional. A honeycomb pattern is chosen in order to provide an equal amount of contingent neighbours for each region, with each neighbour having an equally long border (this would not be the case by using a lattice of squares, which would have the additional difficulty of judging the importance of the different kinds of neighbours ~ queens, bishops or rooks[34] ~ by assigning weights to them). Because the lattice is flat and has a hexagonal shape in itself, there is always one exactly central region. This region has a favourable location, as will become clear from the experiments.

Second, the model is simulated using a space in the shape of a column. In the column the single central region of the lattice is replaced by a belt of regions around the middle of the column. Finally, a globe is modelled. In the globe there is no inherently central location.

Both the column and the globe consist of a honeycomb pattern; in the case of the globe pentagons had to be added (the regions are constructed in the same pattern as on a soccer ball, that is, 12 pentagons and 20 hexagons)[35]. The lattice of honeycombs can be considered similar to a country, whereas the globe could be a model for a world. The column can be seen as an intermediate case, since it replaces the one central region of the lattice by a belt of centrally located regions, whereas on the globe every region is centrally located. Appendix B shows the three spaces considered.

Geographic distance in the artificial geographical spheres is measured by assigning a weight of 1 to neighbouring regions (in the sense that two regions share one border). Regions which do not share a border with a specific region are given a weight by using the concept of nearest neighbours, which means that a different (lower) weight is attributed to a second order neighbour. A second order neighbour does not share a border with a specific region, but does share a border with a neighbour of the specific region. It is very important to notice that no evaluation of relative importance of the connection between regions, based on *ex ante* known information (for

---

[34] These terms are borrowed from chess. A queen is allowed to move in all directions indicating that all 8 neighbours of a square are equally important. A lattice with these characteristics is called a Moore neighbourhood. A bishop is only allowed to move in a diagonal way, while a rook is only allowed to move horizontally or vertically, meaning that one might want to assign a different (lower) weight to neighbours which do not share a border but only one point (the bishop-case) than to neighbours which do share a border (the rook-case). When only neighbours of the rook type are considered, the plane is called a von-Neumann neighbourhood.

[35] It is impossible to construct a three-dimensional figure by the single use of hexagons. Hexagons will always produce a flat sphere, since the sum of the angles of three contingent hexagons is equal to 360 degrees. By adding pentagons the total angle will be less than 360 degrees and will thus produce a three-dimensional figure. It would have been possible to construct a three-dimensional sphere by using pentagons only; however, in that case the total number of pentagons (regions) used would be twelve. The globe that is used in the simulations consists of thirty-two planes (regions), which was considered to give more interesting interactions than a sphere containing only twelve planes.

example the presence of roads and railways) is taken into account. Only geographical distances are reflected. In this way the distance γ_{ij} is determined for every region towards every other region. Now, it is possible to construct a region-by-region matrix of shortest paths. Then, the corresponding weights are determined using the inverse of the orders (inverse shortest path, Hagett, Cliff and Frey, 1977). Note that this way of measuring geographical distance is a special case of $1/(\gamma_{ij}^{x})$ in which x is equal to 1. In the specification of the spillover function (Equation (4.3) of the model in Chapter 4) x was set equal to 1, assuming a simple inverse relationship between geographical distance and knowledge spillovers.

2. VARYING THE IMPACT OF GEOGRAPHICAL DISTANCE

With respect to the resulting pattern of the gaps towards the leader region (for a lattice of honeycombs), the inverse order method leads to a pattern as displayed in Figure 5.1. The numbers within each cell refer to the size of the technology gap a region has towards the leader region. In the next section, we will come back to this pattern. Note that initial knowledge stocks and parameter values are identical across regions[36].

Figure 5.1: Pattern of gaps for the lattice of honeycombs

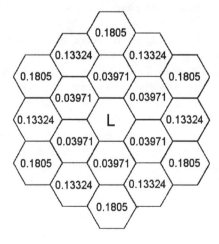

---

[36] The initial values of the data are described in Appendix A.

Knowledge spills over to a region more easily when the distance towards a knowledge-intensive region is small. Since region 1 has the most favourable location, it will end up being the leader (all other things equal).

Figure 5.2 (left): The coefficient of variation for various values of the geographical distance, the lattice
Figure 5.3 (right): The coefficient of variation for various values of the geographical distance, the globe

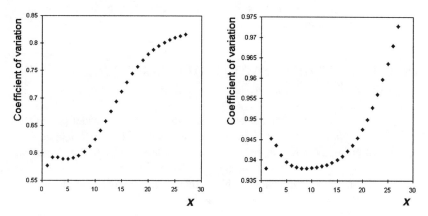

We can add more importance to the geographic distance by increasing the value of x in the relation $1/(\gamma_{ij}^x)^{37}$. Figure 5.2 shows the results for the lattice of honeycombs. The horizontal axis displays the power x. The vertical axis shows the coefficient of variation across the gaps towards the leader at the end of the run. By increasing the influence of geographic distance (x), it is expected that more polarization occurs, and therefore the coefficient of variation goes up. However, Figure 5.2 shows that over the range $x = 3$ to 5, initially the coefficient of variation decreases. An explanation for this is that the two components of the coefficient of variation (the coefficient of variation of the gaps is the ratio between the standard deviation over the gaps toward the leader and the average gap) react in different ways to an increase in the power x. As x is increased from the standard situation $x = 1$ to $x = 2$, both the standard deviation and the average increase (the standard deviation increases more than proportionally to the average), causing the coefficient of variation to rise as well. From $x = 2$ to $x = 4$ the standard deviation and the average continue to rise, although the average increases more than

---

[37] One has to keep in mind that all matrices of weights are scaled to 1000 ($\Sigma_i\Sigma_j\gamma_{ij} = 1000$), therefore making it possible to compare the results across methods and across spheres.

proportionally to the standard deviation, causing the coefficient of variation to decrease in value. From $x = 5$ onwards the average and standard deviation decrease (the average more than the standard deviation), thus the coefficient of variation increases again.

For the lattice of honeycombs, an increase in the power x (geographical distance becomes more important as a factor determining the spillovers across regions) quite quickly (after $x = 5$) leads to higher disparity across the gaps in the regions, indicating a higher degree of polarization. The curve flattens at values of x close to 30, indicating that a further increase in x will cause less polarization.

The column shows different results. Where the coefficient of variation for the lattice seems to stabilize at a certain level when x is increased, the coefficient of variation for the column increases exponentially after an initial decrease (Figure 5.3), indicating that there seems to be no bound to the growth of polarization as a function of x. Note, however, that the increase in polarization may eventually level off for even higher values of x. No experiments to investigate this were conducted.

The globe shows results that are even more interesting. Since the globe consists of relatively many regions compared to the lattice and the column, we only succeeded in taking x up to 3. However, the coefficient of variation is the same for every value of x, $\{x \in \Re | 1 \le x \le 3\}$. Thus, for the globe an increase in importance of the geographical distance in determining the spillovers across regions does not have an impact on the dispersion of the gaps. This observation follows from the specific characteristics of the globe, on which each region can be regarded as being centrally located, that is, the distance from each region to all others is identical. Therefore, an increase in importance of geographical distance will have an identical impact on all regions.

3. VARIATIONS IN THE INITIAL STOCK OF KNOWLEDGE

This section addresses the question whether there is path dependence, in the sense that the resulting gaps at the end of the simulation period (here 10000 time intervals are used) depend on the variation in the initial knowledge stock. To examine this possibility we let the initial knowledge stock of each region vary across runs. All simulations use a Pascal computer program that implements a Runge-Kutta algorithm to numerically solve the differential equations for the technology gap.

3.1 Lattice of honeycombs

By carrying out many simulations (with randomized initial values for the knowledge stock across regions), it is possible to examine the general behaviour of the model. We find that certain patterns in the gaps of the knowledge stocks appear repeatedly.

Figure 5.4: Simulation results based on a lattice of honeycombs

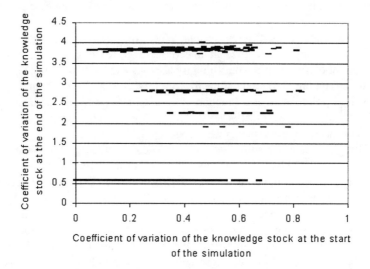

Figure 5.4 displays the results based on a lattice of honeycombs. The horizontal axis represents the coefficient of variation of the knowledge stock at the start of the simulation. The vertical axis represents the coefficient of variation across regions at period 10000.

It appears from the figure that there exists a distribution in five groups. Most prominent are simulations in which the final coefficient of variation has a value around 0.6, simulations in which the final coefficient of variation is about 2.8 and simulations in which the final coefficient of variation is about 3.9. The number of groups that exists decreases when the initial disparity across regions decreases. When the coefficient of variation at the start of the simulation has a value of 0.2 or lower only two groups exist. For an initial disparity of 0.04 (or lower) only one group prevails.

How do these different groupings come about? To answer this question, we have to keep in mind that a higher coefficient of variation indicates a larger dispersion between the gaps towards the leader. A coefficient of variation around 2.8 at the end of the simulation indicates that two regions have fallen behind, that is, display a very large gap towards the leader. A final coefficient of variation around 3.9 indicates that only one region has fallen behind.

Figure 5.5: The pattern of gaps for the lattice of honeycombs

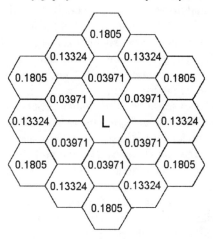

It is notable that all simulations that were performed with an initial coefficient of variation of 0.04 or lower display the same coefficient of variation in the final period, indicating that the same pattern in the gaps occurred in every simulation run after a certain time. In every simulation run, the same leader prevailed and every other region in the lattice had the same gap towards the leader. These gaps are displayed in Figure 5.5. This figure clearly indicates the influence of the geographical distance. The central region has the most favourable position and therefore always prevails as the leader region. The regions located in the first ring around the middle display the lowest gap towards the leader. In the second ring, there is a difference in 'locational advantage'. The regions that have 'a full' honeycomb between the central region and themselves have the largest gap towards the leader. When a straight line is drawn between the central point of such a region and the central point of the centre region, this has the largest length possible in this pattern. Those second ring regions that are located in such way that a straight line drawn between their central point and the centre region is relatively short have a most favourable position. They are located closer to the central region and therefore, on average, get more spillovers than their neighbours on the second ring. The coefficient of variation for this pattern of dispersion is equal to 0.577.

Figure 5.4 shows also that a high initial dispersion across regions in their knowledge stock induces a wide variety in resulting coefficients of variation at the end of the simulation. Identical (large) initial coefficients of variation may lead to different degrees of disparity across runs in the final period. In other words, the initial dispersion cannot exactly determine the distribution of gaps within a single simulation, but it has an influence on the variation in the final coefficient of variation across simulations. Figure 5.4 clearly shows that if the initial coefficient of variation is low, the variety in resulting final coefficients of variation decreases as well. Thus, there seems to be some path dependence (at large initial dispersion).

Why is the model so sensitive to the initial dispersion across regions with respect to their knowledge stock? After the random distribution of knowledge stocks at $t = 0$, the model generates spillovers for every region. With a higher initial dispersion of the knowledge stocks, the probability of a large (initial) gap for one (or more) of the regions is higher. In the case of an initial high gap, the laggard region will barely receive spillovers from the leading region and is likely to fall behind instead of catch up. This implies that the final coefficient of variation for this simulation is quite high. When the initial dispersion across regions is low enough (say 0.04), a lagging region will be able to overcome its technology gap by receiving enough spillovers to prevent falling behind. Thus, for several values of the initial coefficient of variation, no region will fall behind and the gaps at period 10000 will show the pattern as displayed in Figure 5.5.

Table 5.1: Percentage of regions falling behind

Range out of which the initial knowledge stock of each region is taken (at random)	Percentage of runs that show regions falling behind (out of 50 runs)
Range 1 –2	0
Range 0.5 – 2	0
Range 0.1 – 2	16
Range 0.01 – 2	68
Range 0 – 2	74

Table 5.1 confirms this argumentation. In the present experiment, the knowledge stock for each individual region is drawn from a uniform

distribution, from which the lower boundary is shifted upwards, while the upper boundary remains constant. Table 5.1 displays in the first column the boundaries of the uniform distribution. This gives an indication of the variation in the initial knowledge stock across regions. The second column displays the percentage of runs in the range containing regions that fell behind. This table points to the conclusion that the number of runs in which falling behind occurs increases as the initial range is increased and there is a higher probability of a large variation in the initial knowledge stocks.

Figure 5.6: The net spillover between two regions

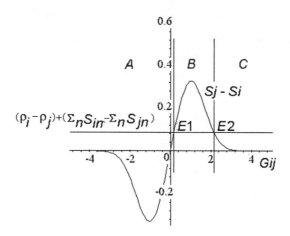

Figure 5.6 shows how this happens. The curve in Figure 5.6 displays the net spillover function between two regions, the leader region versus another one (the geographical distance between the two regions is equal to three in this figure). A small variety in initial knowledge stocks implies that all regions start from a position in range *A* or *B* (the catch-up area, the region will undergo dynamic forces that move it along the curve towards equilibrium *E*1), but never *C* (the falling behind area, dynamic forces will cause the gap towards the leader to increase). At a high initial disparity across regions, the chance is enlarged that regions will start at a position located in *C*. Therefore some regions will fall behind and 'disturb' the pattern in Figure 5.5.

Of course there are other factors that determine the location of equilibrium point *E*2, which is the border between catching up and falling behind. Equation (4.5') in Chapter 4 showed that the terms $(\rho_i - \rho_j)$ and $(\Sigma_n S_{in} - \Sigma_n S_{jn})$, together, determine the position of the horizontal line in Figure 5.6.

Therefore, a movement in the horizontal line (and therefore in the horizontal position of $E2$) can be caused by two factors. First a variation in the difference between the exogenous rates of growth of the knowledge stocks of two regions. In the experiment we consider in this section, this factor is equal to zero, since we assume that the rate of exogenous growth of the knowledge stock is equal across regions. Second, a difference across regions in the spillovers received from all other regions. For this term, the favourability of the geographic location of a region is crucial, as was confirmed by Figure 5.5.

3.2 A column

In the previous section, the regions located in the centre or in the ring around the centre had a locational advantage with respect to receiving knowledge spillovers. This is partly reproduced in the present set of simulations, which use a column as the spatial structure.

Figure 5.7: The pattern of gaps on a column

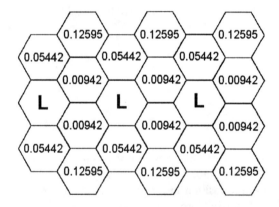

Figure 5.7 corresponds to 5.5. It displays the case for which no falling behind takes place. The regions located in the middle band of the column have the most favourable position with respect to receiving spillovers from neighbouring regions, because they have more neighbours with a low order than the regions on the edge of the column. As said before, the more neighbours a region has with a relative low order, the more potential spillovers it will receive.

Figure 5.8: Simulation results based on a column

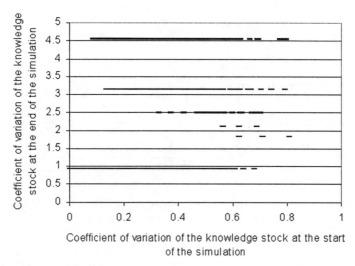

Figure 5.8 shows the sensitivity of this sphere to variations in the initial knowledge stocks across regions. Again, the disparity at the start of the simulation is plotted against the disparity at the end of the simulation. Six groupings are visible, at different values on the vertical axis from those in the lattice. This is due to the fact that the dynamics of this sphere lead to a different final outcome of the model, namely the one presented in Figure 5.7 (for example, three leaders instead of one in the case of the lattice). The disparity of the gaps across regions as displayed by Figure 5.7 becomes unique when at the start of the simulation there is little disparity across knowledge stocks, that is, the initial coefficient of variation has a value of 0.1 or lower. This is the case at the utmost left of Figure 5.8.

3.3 A globe

For the final experiment in this set, the regions are located on a globe. In this sphere, all hexagon-shaped regions have an equal potential for receiving knowledge spillovers. The same holds for all pentagon-shaped regions. However, a hexagon-shaped region has a small advantage over a pentagon-shaped region with respect to receiving knowledge spillovers, since the honeycomb shape provides a region with six instead of five direct neighbours and thus probably more spillovers.

Figure 5.9: The pattern of gaps based on a globe

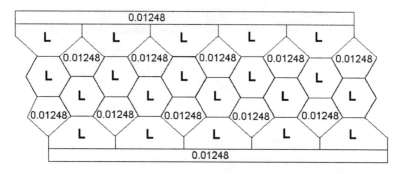

Similar to the experiments carried out with the lattice and the column, several simulations based on this sphere were performed. One single pattern of gaps toward the leader occurred at low initial disparity of the knowledge stocks. This pattern is displayed in Figure 5.9. In this pattern, every hexagon-shaped region became a leader eventually, and every pentagon-shaped region developed a gap towards the leader of size 0.01248. This result indicates that hexagon-shaped regions indeed have a small locational advantage compared to pentagon-shaped regions, with respect to receiving knowledge spillovers.

Figure 5.10: Simulation results based on a globe

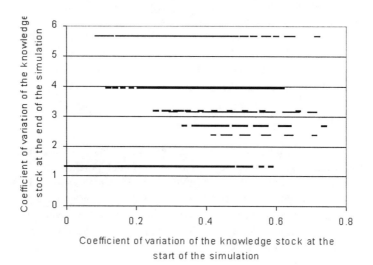

Figure 5.11: Coefficient of variation corresponding to the number of regions that fall behind

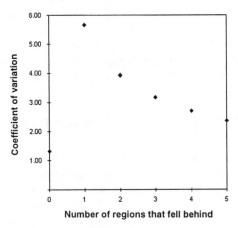

Figure 5.10 gives an illustration of the average coefficient of variation over the gaps towards the leader in period 10000 in every run. The figure shows that when the initial disparity increases from 0 to about 0.6, the number of different groupings increases, until there are six different groupings at an initial coefficient of variation of 0.6. Each of these six different groupings corresponds to a unique number of regions that fell behind during the simulation run. This is illustrated by Figure 5.11.

Figure 5.10 indicates that at a large initial disparity across regions several situations occur. In the most extreme case, five regions fall behind. As the initial disparity decreases, the emphasis shifts to situations in which little regions fall behind. Finally, (coefficient of variation is equal to about 0.1) the model arrives at a situation in which no regions fall behind and the dispersion of the gaps displays the pattern shown in Figure 5.9 at period 10000.

3.4 Summary and conclusion

In this section, the disparity across the knowledge stock of each region at the start of the simulation was plotted against the disparity in knowledge stocks resulting at the end of the simulation. It was shown that the resulting disparity in gaps across runs is sensitive to the initial disparity across knowledge stocks. For each sphere, there is a certain interval in which no falling behind of regions will occur. When there is no falling behind, the influence of geographic distance on the model becomes clearest. The lattice shows the typical resulting pattern with the centrally located region being the leader.

The geographical distance towards the central region determines the gap of all other regions. The column is characterized by a belt of leaders. The globe has many leaders, since all hexagon-shaped regions have the same favourable geographic location for receiving spillovers from other regions.

Thus, if there is no falling behind, each run in each geographical sphere locks in to a certain chain of events, which in the end will lead to a pattern of gaps that is solely determined by geographical distances. Falling behind may 'disturb' this pattern, and lead to higher disparity.

4. VARIATIONS IN THE LEARNING CAPABILITY

In this set of experiments a randomly generated learning capability (δ) is assigned to each region. The value for δ is drawn from a uniform distribution for which the upper boundary and lower boundary are determined by calibration (Table 5.2). Several sets of 50 runs with different ranges were generated[38]. Table 5.2 gives some statistical information on the results.

Table 5.2: Average, standard deviation and coefficient of variation of the gap over all regions (50 runs)

	0 to 2	0 to 10	0 to 50	1 to 10	1 to 2	2 to 3	40 to 41
Average	1.562	1.562	1.562	1.901	0.543	0.543	0.580
Standard deviation	0.435	0.435	0.435	0.578	0.088	0.078	0.016
Coefficient of variation	0.278	0.278	0.278	0.304	0.161	0.144	0.028

A number of conclusions can be drawn from this table. First, we observe that the range in which the learning capability is allowed to vary should be small in order to have a low coefficient of variation. Second, the interval should be small *relative* to the level of the learning capability. If the interval 1 to 2 is compared with 2 to 3 and 40 to 41, it can be seen that the coefficient of variation decreases over these intervals.

This is quite intuitive, since a relatively large difference in learning capabilities means that regions cannot implement the knowledge spilled over from other regions. This is illustrated in Figure 4.7, in which a relatively large difference in learning capabilities among two regions causes a skewness of the spillover curve, so that it becomes very difficult for the backward region to catch up.

---

[38] The calibration shown applies to the lattice of honeycombs. Calibrations for the other spheres indicated that the choice of a different sphere does influence the calibration.

Figure 5.12: Frequency diagram of the coefficient of variation at the end of the run based on a lattice

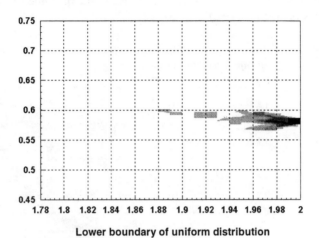

Lower boundary of uniform distribution

Figure 5.13: Frequency diagram of the coefficient of variation at the end of the run based on a column

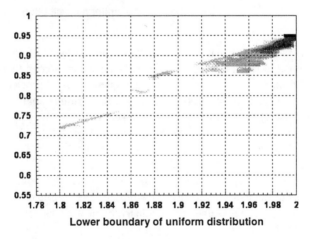

Lower boundary of uniform distribution

The sensitivity to the lower boundary for the lattice is shown in Figure 5.12. In this figure the value for δ is drawn from a uniform distribution with upper boundary 2, and lower boundary varying from 1.8 to 2, taking steps of 0.01. The lower boundary is displayed on the horizontal axis. On the vertical axis, the coefficient of variation of the resulting technology gaps over all regions (after 10000 simulated time periods) is shown. The shades in the figure correspond to frequencies over the 50 runs, with complete black corresponding to a frequency of 50 (that is, all runs). White shades indicate very low (sometimes zero) frequencies.

Figure 5.14: Frequency diagram of the coefficient of variation at the end of the run based on a globe

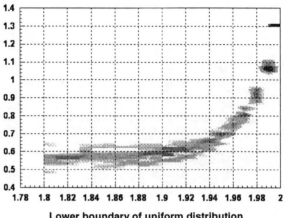

Lower boundary of uniform distribution

It has to be noted that in none of these ranges does falling behind occur, that is, an equilibrium value of the gap always exists. Recall that the higher δ for a region, the more it is capable to implement the knowledge that spills over from other regions. Regions with a high learning capability make more effective use of the knowledge they receive.

For the column (Figure 5.13) and the globe (Figure 5.14) the same analysis is done. A number of striking features emerge from these three figures. The coefficient of variation for the lattice is comet-shaped. The trail of 'the comet' (the dark spot at the right of the figures) disperses equally to all directions as the lower boundary is decreased. The coefficient of variation for the column does the same, but exclusively in a downward direction. The globe does not show such a clear fan-shape. In this case, there is only a little dispersion on the left-hand side of the curve, but the coefficient of variation across the ranges shows the same downward-sloping trend (from right to left) as the column.

This last result is counterintuitive. A higher diversity across regions (in terms of the initial learning capability) causes lower levels of disparity in the resulting gaps at the end of the simulation, whereas less initial diversity leads to more disparity in knowledge stocks.

What causes the dispersion in the trail of 'the comet' in the figures for the lattice and the column? When the range is limited to only one value (in this case 2), the only factor that has an influence on the difference between regions is the geographical distance. As was seen before, distance is a polarizing factor and leads to a distribution of gaps for the lattice as displayed in Figure 5.5 and a distribution of gaps for the column as displayed in Figure 5.7. When the range is broadened, a second polarizing factor executes an influence on the regions, namely the learning capability. These two polarizing factors counteract. A region with an unfavourable geographical location may (randomly) obtain a high learning capability, while the centrally located region may (randomly) obtain a low learning capability. This leads to lower levels of disparity *within* one run, but also leads to more disparity *across* the runs. Since there is more opportunity for the learning capability as a second polarizing factor with larger ranges (at the left end of the figure), the outcomes ~ in terms of coefficient of variation across the gaps ~ of different runs become more distinct, causing the fan-shape in the lattice and the column.

This does not yet explain why the figures for the column (5.13) and globe (5.14) show an upward slope, and the lattice does not. The difference between the spheres lies mainly in the fact that the column and globe have three or more regions that will become leader in the end (if only geographic forces are considered). In addition to these leaders, there are a number of regions which display a very small gap towards the leaders. For the lattice there is only one region which becomes a leader. The six first-ring regions have a gap that is relatively large.

This means that in the case of a globe or column, there are more than one 'neighbourhoods', with 'local' leaders. When such a 'local' leader is affected by a low learning capability (which is more likely for larger ranges of this parameter), this not only affects the local leader, but indeed the whole neighbourhood. This causes an overall lower coefficient of variation. On the other hand, a lower coefficient of variation could be the result of higher learning capabilities for the peripheral regions. However, the chance that all (or at least a large part) of the peripheral regions (randomly) obtain(s) a higher learning capability than the potential local leaders is limited. The impact of differences in learning capability grows disproportionally with the range, causing the upward-sloping pattern in Figures 5.13 and 5.14. Since the globe has more potential local leaders than the column (20 versus 3), the chance is higher in the case of the globe that a local leader (randomly) obtains a low learning capability. Therefore, Figure 5.14 displays a higher upward slope than Figure 5.13.

What is also peculiar in Figure 5.14 is the typical curve the coefficient of variation displays when the lower boundary is decreased. From 1.9 downwards there seems to be a horizontal trend. This can be explained as follows. At the left-hand side of the figure, the randomness in the parameter apparently reaches a level at which additional randomness does not increase the chance that an additional potential local leader obtains a relatively low learning capability. Therefore, the number of potential local leaders does not decrease any further at larger parameter ranges, resulting in the horizontal area in the figure.

The conclusion that can be drawn from these figures (5.13 and 5.14) is an extraordinary one. Contrary to what is generally assumed, it is found that when differences in learning capabilities increase across regions, the disparity between them decreases. This is a direct effect from the inclusion of geographical distance in the model. Thus, the results show that leaving out distance from a model of technology gaps may indeed lead to rather special results.

5. VARIATIONS IN THE EXOGENOUS RATE OF GROWTH OF THE KNOWLEDGE STOCK

In the following set of experiments the exogenous rate of growth of the knowledge stock is randomly chosen from different ranges, while the initial knowledge stocks (as well as other parameters) of the regions are equal. Compared to the first set of experiments, in which the knowledge stock was initially random, this set behaves a little differently. In general, it does matter for final leadership whether a region has an initial advantage. The region which becomes a leader early on will, in most of the cases, remain in this position.

Two determinants of leadership in the first stages of the simulation occur. On the one hand, the initial exogenous rate of growth of the knowledge stock is a very important influence in determining the leader in the first periods of simulation. However, the geographical distance to centrally located regions has not to be taken for granted, since geographic forces rule the amount of spillovers received by all regions. In general, the region that has the highest ρ of all centrally located first order regions (which receive many spillovers due to their geographic location) will most likely become a leader.

Figure 5.15: Frequency diagram of the coefficient of variation at the end of the run based on a lattice

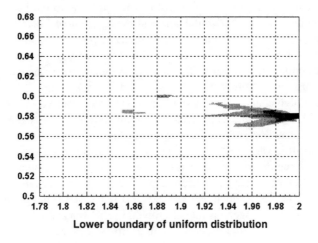

Lower boundary of uniform distribution

Figure 5.16: Frequency diagram of the coefficient of variation at the end of the run based on a column

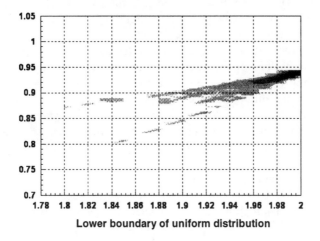

Lower boundary of uniform distribution

This can be explained by looking again at Equation (4.5') in Section 3. The term $(\rho_i - \rho_j)$; together with the term $(\Sigma_n S_{in} - \Sigma_n S_{jn})$, determines the position of the horizontal line in Figure 5.6. In the foregoing experiments the term $(\rho_i - \rho_j)$ was equal to zero, in this experiment ρ is randomly chosen out of different ranges. It can easily be understood that if the difference between the exogenous rates of growth of the knowledge stock across regions is small, the horizontal line in Figure 5.6 will be located close to the horizontal axis. This implies that the horizontal line and the S_j–S_i curve intersect at the two equilibrium points of which the right one has a position relatively far to the right of the top of the spillover curve. Therefore, regions can catch up even at a large initial gap towards the leader. A small difference between the exogenous rates of growth of the knowledge stock in the lattice therefore implies a high chance of a distribution of gaps as displayed in Figure 5.5 (in which all regions catch up) occurring. However, if every region is able to catch up, that does not necessarily mean that the pattern of Figure 5.5 is produced. It is very well possible in this experiment that a region other than the central region will end up with final leadership, and all other regions will catch up to their stable equilibrium gap towards this leader region.

In order to see in which way the model is sensitive to changes in the range out of which the exogenous rate of growth was chosen at random, several sets of 50 runs were carried out, each with a different range. Figure 5.15 shows the results for the lattice when the lower boundary of the range is increased from 1.8 to 2 with steps of 0.01. The upper boundary is held constant at 2. The vertical axis shows the coefficient of variation over the last period in every run. This figure illustrates that only for a very small interval do all 50 observations show nearly the same coefficient of variation.

The coefficient of variation displays a fan-shape (identical to the experiment with the learning capability). All coefficients of variation tend to one value as the gap between lower and upper boundary decreases. The explanation is the same as in the experiment with the learning capability. Increasing the difference in exogenous rates of growth of the knowledge stock introduces a second polarizing factor, next to geographic distance. The two polarizing factors counteract, thereby causing a larger equality across gaps *within* one run and a larger disparity across coefficients of variation *across* several (50) runs.

For the column, the sensitivity to the lower boundary of the interval is given in 5.16. Contrary to the lattice this sphere seems to generate mostly coefficients of variation which are smaller than the one in which three leaders appear (the dark spot at the right of the figure)[39]. Again a fan-shape appears. The explanation for these features is the same as that for the case in which the learning capability was varied across ranges. The fan-shape is generated by the growing inequality in the coefficient of variation across runs, as the

---

[39] Figure 5.7 shows the distribution of the gaps across regions which occurs at the extreme right of the figure.

difference in learning capabilities across regions counteracts the difference in geographic location (from right to left). The line is upward sloping because within each run the disparity across gaps increases, as the range is decreased, due to the characteristics of the column.

The figure for the globe (5.17) shows a curve that is upward sloping and shows less of a fan-shape. There is only little dispersion at the left-hand side of the curve. Contrary to the former experiment with the learning capability, this curve does not yet show a horizontal area when the gap between lower and upper boundary is large. However, we see that the lowest observation has a coefficient of variation of about 0.6 at a lower boundary of 1.4. If the lower boundary were to be decreased further, the figure would start to show a horizontal trend.

Figure 5.17: Frequency diagram of the coefficient of variation at the end of the run based on a globe

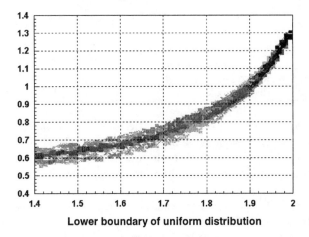

Lower boundary of uniform distribution

The general conclusion from this section follows the same directions as the former section in which the learning capability of each region was varied. The patterns in this section show similar trends, although there are a few differences. The graph for the column, under a variation of the exogenous rate of growth, shows the same fan-shape, but the upward trend is much less steep than under a variation in the learning capability in the former section. This indicates that a variation in the learning capability has a stronger counteracting effect (to geographical distance) than a variation in the exogenous rate of growth of the knowledge stock. If the range in which a parameter can vary is small, larger differences occur across runs in the case of the learning capability compared to the exogenous rate of growth of the knowledge stock.

Virtually the same holds for the globe. The effect of the learning capability on overall disparity is larger than in the experiment in which the exogenous rate of growth of the knowledge stock was varied in the same range.

6. SUMMARY AND CONCLUSIONS

This chapter presented the simulation results for the spillover model as discussed in Chapter 4. From the simulations executed until now, we can draw several conclusions. Certain structures appear when different kinds of simulations are compared. Table 5.3 allocates the findings into four groups that show similar characteristics.

Table 5.3: Summary of the results

	Lattice	Column	Globe
Variations in the initial knowledge stock	A		
Variations in the learning capability	B	C	D
Variations in the exogenous rate of growth of the knowledge stock			

The cases A show that if initial differences in knowledge stocks across regions are small enough, no falling behind occurs. The system locks in to an evolution of events, which leads to an equilibrium state in which geographical proximity is the only determinant of the size of the gaps of the regions.

B, C and D show cases in which parameter changes have an effect on disparity. We can discriminate the results according to geographic sphere. The lattice generates the following characteristics of the results. The more differences there are across regions with regard to learning capability and exogenous rate of growth of the knowledge stock, the larger is the variation in resulting gaps. The runs can show both higher and lower disparity than the 'perfect' distribution of gaps as regions initially have more differences.

We see a clear difference in the situation under B compared with the situation under C, which concerns the column. In C, the case in which all regions are equal to each other generates the highest disparity. As soon as regions show differences with respect to the learning capability or the exogenous rate of growth, the disparity becomes less. In this case, there are no runs that have a larger coefficient of variation than the equilibrium distribution of case A.

The globe (D) shows a slightly different effect to the change in parameters. The disparity decreases as regions show larger differences in the value of their parameter. In this respect, these results are similar to those for the column. However, if a certain minimum level of disparity is reached, the disparity will not decrease any further. Larger initial differences in parameters will induce results which have a similar coefficient of variation.

Thus, varying a level variable such as the initial knowledge stock has a different kind of effect than varying a parameter (which influences the growth rates). The first one causes geographic proximity to become the main influence as regions become more equal, whereas the latter shows that there are two counteracting forces at work. Increasing differences in the learning capability and the exogenous rate of growth of the knowledge stock are in themselves polarizing factors. Combined with geographic forces, however, they lead to less disparity across regions.

From a policy perspective, the learning capability of a region can be influenced by actively trying to enhance the knowledge infrastructure of a region. Stimulating cooperation between firms and research organizations, and ameliorating the educational structure, are measures that have this effect. However, from this study it appears that the existence of differences across regions may not be as 'bad' as is generally believed. The mere existence of differences in learning capabilities across regions may cause disparity between regions to be relatively small.

With respect to the exogenous rate of growth of the knowledge stock of a region, this could be enhanced by stimulation of the R&D activities in a region. In fact, there are several policy measures that aim at stimulating (private) R&D. Again, the present model points out that small differences across regions in their exogenous rate of growth of the knowledge stock may lead to relatively large differences across regions with respect to gaps in the knowledge stock.

APPENDIX A: DEFAULT LEVELS OF THE VARIABLES AND VALUES OF THE PARAMETERS

Number of periods, t	10000
Knowledge stock, K	10
Exogenous rate of growth of the knowledge stock, ρ	1
Learning capability δ	1
Catch-up parameter, μ	1
β	0.005
α	0.005
Verdoorn parameter, λ	1

Geographical distance, γ, is constructed with the help of three different types of distance tables, one for each sphere.

APPENDIX B: GEOGRAPHICAL STRUCTURES

Figure 5.18 (left): Lattice of honeycombs
Figure 5.19 (right): A column

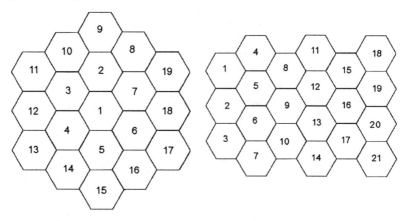

Figure 5.18 displays the topography of the regions on a lattice of honey-combs. The number within each hexagon was used to establish the geographical distances between all hexagons. Figure 5.19 displays the

column. Region 1 borders regions 4, 5 and 2 as well as 18 and 19; region 2 borders regions 1, 5, 6 and 3 as well as 19 and 20; and region 3 besides regions 2, 6 and 7 also has regions 20 and 21 as its direct neighbours. Thus if one were to walk from region 20 to the right, one would reappear at the left of the figure in region 2 or 3.

The figure below (Figure 5.20) represents a globe with 12 pentagons and 20 hexagons. For the graphical representation, we used the same principle that was applied in making a map of the world. Hence, the regions close to the poles look larger than they actually are, while the regions around the equator show their true proportions. At the bottom and the top are regions 29 and 9. These are pentagons, for example region 9 borders five regions, namely 3, 2, 8, 10 and 11. Region 29 and 9 are in reality as large as region 1. The graphic representation of a globe also has the consequence of making region 3 seem to differ in size from region 6. Again, this is not the case in reality, region 3 is an ordinary hexagon. The same goes for all the other regions bordering 9 or 29. It should also be noted that region 11 not only borders regions 9, 10, 24, 25 and 12, but also region 3. Similarly, region 12 also borders regions 3 and 4, region 13 has regions 4 and 14 as direct neighbours as well, whereas region 28 also shares a border with regions 14 and 15.

Figure 5.20: A globe

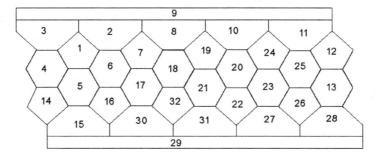

6. Modelling Technology Spillovers, Introducing Countries

The model that will be presented in this chapter can be viewed as an elaboration of the model in the previous chapter. In the former model regions were assumed to coexist in a world without national borders. A complete unification of the involved economies prevailed. In fact, no distinction was made between countries. The model in this chapter gives a more adequate representation of reality, in that it distinguishes between countries by introducing (among other things) an exchange rate system. A labour market and capital accumulation are also added in this extended version of the model.

These changes make it possible to focus on the economic relations between countries in addition to interregional knowledge spillovers. Only the latter aspect was the focus of the previous chapter. This elaboration also allows us to explore the influence of economic integration on the distribution of knowledge and growth across regions.

The main economic content will be taken from the Goodwin model, as described briefly in Chapter 3. Section 1 discusses arguments for the introduction of countries into the model. This section is followed by a description of the extended model (2.1) and the verification of this model (2.2). Section 3 is directed to the simulation results. The first part of this section (3.1) focuses on the introduction of a monetary union[40], while the second part (3.2) deals with barriers to knowledge spillovers. Section 4 concludes and summarizes the main findings of this chapter.

1. WHY INTRODUCE COUNTRIES ?

In what respect does the introduction of countries enrich the model? By abstracting from countries, the model in the former chapter refrained from

---

[40] The terms 'monetary union' and 'system of fixed exchange rates' will be used interchangeably, since in terms of the model a system of fixed exchange rates is identical to a monetary union. Both refer to a situation in which each currency can be denominated in the currency of another country against a fixed rate.

taking into account barriers to trade and barriers to knowledge spillovers. These barriers can have an important influence on the distribution of growth across regions. First, trade can have an influence on growth by enhancing specialization and thus enabling increasing returns to scale. Various trade-growth models explore this relation (Grossman and Helpman, 1990). Second, international specialization may have an impact on the amount of spillovers that take place within a country relative to the amount between countries. Thus, barriers to trade and to knowledge spillovers may well have an influence on the distribution of gaps throughout all regions.

Traditional trade theory explains differences in production structures mainly through differences in underlying characteristics (endowments or technologies). In the Heckscher-Olin explanation of international trade, trade is driven by comparative advantage based on factor endowment differences. In the classical Ricardian theory, industry-wide differences in technology endorse trade (Flam, 1992). New trade theory explains differences in production structures through differences in underlying characteristics as well, but focuses on increasing returns to scale and allows imperfect competition and, moreover, countries are assumed to specialize in industries where they have economies of scale[41]. Consequently, geographic concentration of production will occur. Economies of scale are essential for explaining the uneven geographical distribution of economic activity. Economic integration leads to larger markets and therefore to economies of scale. This results in specialization and polarization of economic activity (Ottaviano and Puga, 1997).

Within the broad stream of new trade-growth models, three currents can be distinguished (Dowrick, 1997): neo-Smithian models emphasizing that trade enables specialization which ~ through learning by doing ~ yields increased productivity. Every activity in which a country is specialized has the same possibilities for growth. Only the geographic distribution of growth per sector is influenced by trade. The gains from trade liberalization are spread evenly in this theory. Neo-Ricardian models focus on specialization in particular activities, induced by comparative advantage. Countries will specialize in certain activities according to their comparative advantage. However, activities can have different growth rates. Therefore, countries will grow faster if the activities in which they are specialized are characterized by higher rates of productivity. Again, the geographic distribution of growth

---

[41] This is true for models that are constructed along the lines of the Marshallian approach. It is assumed that industry-specific externalities (Marshallian externalities) exist. The Chamberlinian approach, on the other hand, assumes product differentiation. In this approach countries specialize in different versions of the same product. In this section we limit the overview to models that contain Marshallian externalities.

differs per sector, but this theory goes even further: a disparity in overall growth can emerge because different sectors have different rates of productivity. Economic integration could have the consequence that some countries end up having low growth, because their comparative advantage lies in low growth activities. Finally, neo-Millian theories emphasize the role of trade as a channel for international diffusion of ideas and technology. Imitation, reverse engineering and direct exchange of ideas between buyers and sellers ~ all inherent to trade ~ causes an effective distribution of knowledge throughout the world. International trade enhances knowledge spillovers across country borders. Trade liberalization would therefore increase output for all economies involved.

Quantitative studies along these lines have focused on samples of countries throughout the world (not specific EU countries) and have indicated a positive relationship between trade liberalization and growth. The results suggest that gains of the order of 0.5 percentage points per year (in terms of growth rates) might be expected (Dowrick, 1997).

To be able to study these influences, the situation under barriers to trade and knowledge spillovers has to be compared to a situation in which these barriers are released. In other words, comparing a situation before and after economic integration will make it possible to explore the effects of trade barriers on the distribution of growth. Pelkmans (1997, p. 2) defines economic integration as: 'the elimination of economic frontiers between two or more economies. In turn, an economic frontier is any demarcation over which actual and potential mobilities of goods, services and production factors, as well as communication flows, are relatively low.' Economic frontiers can have different forms. Balassa (1975) describes the different stages of economic integration. In each of these stages one sort of economic frontier is released. At first tariffs and quotas are removed. One of the final stages of integration is the introduction of a monetary union (pegging the exchange rates).

It is difficult to make a clear-cut distinction between barriers to trade and barriers to knowledge spillovers. International barriers to trade come in various formats. Exchange rate volatility (Section 3.1), quotas, tariffs and a politically unstable situation all form a barrier to international trade. Under the (Millian) assumption that trade in goods is accompanied by diffusion of knowledge (every product contains information about for instance its construction that can be deduced by reverse engineering) a barrier to cross-country trade can limit the knowledge spillovers in these directions. However, trade is one (indirect) way in which knowledge is diffused.

In this chapter, the focus will lie on removing trade barriers by introducing a monetary union. The model developed in this chapter will take into account increasing returns, through the Verdoorn effect. Specialization will not be deepened as a source of disparity across regions, since only one sector will be introduced. Although the focus will lie on the effect of (releasing the) barriers to trade, one section will be devoted to barriers to knowledge spillovers.

2. DESCRIPTION OF THE MODEL

2.1 Extension of the model

This section will concentrate on the extension of the model compared to the model presented in the former chapters. The economy consists of a number of countries (denoted by $j = 1..m$), each of which contains several regions (denoted by $i = 1..n_j$). Only one good is produced (specialization is ruled out). Demand for the good is assumed to be determined by the number of people (denoted by N), labour productivity (defined by $a = Q/L$, in which Q denotes production and L denotes the number people who have a job) and the world price in terms of the home currency (eP, e denotes the exchange rate and P the world price) for the good. Increasing labour productivity is assumed to have a positive influence on demand, since it gives an indication of a relatively high general level of development of the economy[42]. The demand function is given by the following equation:

$$D_{ij} = \frac{d_{ij} N_{ij} a_{ij}}{e_j P},$$ (6.1)

in which d is a parameter.

Supply is assumed to be inelastic in the short run, so that it can be set equal to productive capacity (Q). Capital is homogeneous. Assuming a fixed coefficients production technology, labour demand is simply a function of the capital stock in the sector. We assume one world price for the good, which can be found by confronting world demand with world supply:

$$\sum_{j=1}^{m} \sum_{i=1}^{n} \frac{d_{ij} N_{ij} a_{ij}}{e_j P} = \sum_{j=1}^{m} \sum_{i=1}^{n} l_{ij} N_{ij} a_{ij},$$ (6.2)

---

[42] Of course, it should be noted that this holds only for a certain group of goods, namely goods that satisfy the non-primary needs (normal goods). For instance, people will always need food, independent of the development of the economy.

where the share of total population employed in region i of country j is defined as $l_{ij} = L_{ij}/N_{ij}$ (L is labour demand, equal to $C/(ac)$, where C is the capital stock, and the capital output ratio $c \equiv C/Q$ is assumed to be a fixed parameter). When (initial) levels for C, N, a and e are given, this equation can be solved for the world price P as follows:

$$P = \frac{\displaystyle\sum_{j=1}^{m}\sum_{i=1}^{n}\frac{d_{ij}N_{ij}}{e_j}}{\displaystyle\sum_{j=1}^{m}\sum_{i=1}^{n}L_{ij}}.$$

(6.3)

The growth of labour productivity is assumed to be proportional to the growth of the knowledge stock:

$$\hat{a}_{ij} = \xi \hat{K}_{ij},$$

(6.4)

in which ξ is a parameter which is set equal to one in the following experiments. The spillover system, which determines the knowledge stock of each region at each moment in time, is unaltered compared to the model in the former chapter.

Next, we define capital accumulation. The 'real' profit rate (profits as a share of the capital stock) is defined as follows:

$$r_{ij} = \frac{e_j P Q_{ij} - w_{ij} L_{ij}}{e_j P C_{ij}} = \frac{1}{c}\left(1 - \frac{w_{ij}}{a_{ij} e_j P}\right),$$

(6.5)

where w is the nominal wage rate (measured in domestic currency). We assume that all profits are reinvested in capital in the same region, and that the price for capital equipment is equal to the world price of output. Thus, the growth rate of the capital stocks can be written as:

$$\hat{C} = r_{ij}.$$

(6.6)

Now, we add the dynamics of the exchange rates. The value of the trade balance measured in foreign currency per sector is equal to the difference between the country's production and its consumption, that is:

$$B_j = P(Q_j - D_j).$$

(6.7)

The assumption is that the growth of the exchange rate depends on the value of the trade balance as a fraction of the value of total GDP (both measured in current prices and foreign currency). More specifically, we assume that the following equation holds:

$$\hat{e}_j = \varepsilon \left(\frac{B_j}{PQ_j} - \frac{B^*}{PQ^*} \right),$$

(6.8)

where ε (>0) is a parameter. The superscript * indicates the reference country for which the growth in the exchange rate is equal to zero, ($\hat{e} = 0$, $e = 1$). This formulation ensures certain basic characteristics with regard to consistency. For example, a change of the reference country (that is to say, expressing all values for all countries in the currency of a different country) does not change the growth rates of the exchange rates using the above equation. Also, note that the exchange rate between two countries of which neither is the reference country can be calculated by dividing their exchange rates relative to the reference country. Thus, for m countries, one can calculate all remaining ($m^2 - m$)/2 exchange rates if the m exchange rates relative to one reference country are known. The above equation for the dynamics of the exchange rate ensures that changing the reference country does not change the resulting values of the exchange rate growth rates.

The labour market is characterized by a Phillips curve, determining the growth of the nominal wage rate:

$$\hat{w} = -m + n \frac{L_{ij}}{N_{ij}},$$

(6.9)

in which m and n are parameters. Population (N) is assumed to grow at a fixed rate η.

2.2 Verification of the model

In essence, the model works as follows. The regions converge to a steady state, in which all regions have a certain gap towards the leader region (in terms of knowledge), see Figure 6.1 (stable equilibrium point $E1$). If a region has converged to its steady state equilibrium, its gap towards the leader region does not change any more. This is analogous to the situation in the model in the former chapter. In this steady state, profit rates (and hence unit labour costs) are equal across regions, ensuring equal growth rates. Possible differences in the three factors defining unit labour costs (profit rates), that is, labour productivity, the exchange rate, and the (nominal) wage rate will offset each other. Differences in labour productivity arise from the knowledge spillover system, the Verdoorn effect and exogenous differences in the world price. Exchange rates may operate at the level of a country, whereas wages were assumed to be specific for regions.

Figure 6.1: The net spillover curve

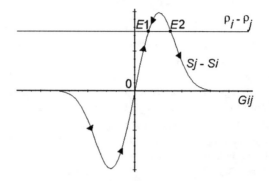

The introduction of a monetary union has the consequence that exchange rate adjustments are no longer possible. Therefore, an asymmetric situation regarding competitiveness can only be compensated by a change in wages.

Figures 6.2 and 6.3: Geographic structure with a border between countries

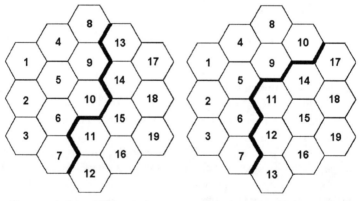

In the remainder of this section, some experiments will be carried out to illustrate the working of the model. The experiments are based on the honeycomb structure in which a border is drawn to divide the plain in two groups of regions: the two countries. This can be done in several ways. Here we show two alternatives. Figures 6.2 and 6.3 show two geographic structures. In both figures regions 1 to 10 make up the first country, which is the largest, and regions 11 to 19 make up the smaller second country. The two geographic structures differ in whether the largest country contains the overall centrally located region. This might give different resulting gaps, because this region is the most favourable for receiving knowledge spillovers. The experiments so far, however, seem to show that these two different geographic structures do not cause differences in the resulting gaps[43]. This is probably because the regional differences in labour productivity do not influence the exchange rate. Therefore, it does not really matter whether the smallest or the largest country contains the central region. In the remainder of this chapter, the second geographic structure will be used, in which the central region is located in the smallest country.

Figure 6.4: Gaps per region under flexible exchange rates in the case of no falling behind

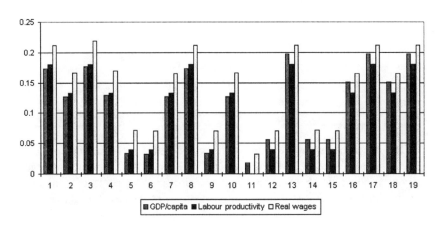

Figure 6.4 shows that the *real* regional wage rates (w_i /eP) form an image that follows the trends in the disparity in labour productivity. This figure depicts the average gap over the last 100 periods. Regions with a high gap with respect to labour productivity also have a high gap in real wages. The gaps reflect the geographic location of the regions. The central region (region 11, see the structure for the lattice of honeycombs) has the lowest (average) gap with respect to all variables. Note that the gap with respect to GDP per

---

[43] This holds for experiments with respect to barriers to trade. In Section 3.2 will be shown that the country containing the overall centrally located region experiences less disparity.

capita and real wages in the central region is not equal to zero. This is due to the fact that these variables behave in a cyclical manner. Since the cycles of the different regions are generally in different phases, leadership (with respect to GDP per capita[44] and real wages) switches quite often, which results in an average positive value of the gap. The cycle in real wages has an amplitude which is larger than the amplitude of the cycle in GDP per capita, therefore real wages show a larger average gap than the other variables.

Next, we focus on regions that are falling behind and have not converged to the steady state $E1$ in Figure 6.1, but instead are moving over time along the arrow at the right side of the figure. Their gaps toward the leader region keep increasing. The resulting effect on the components of the unit labour costs are reported in Table 6.1.

Table 6.1: Flexible exchange rates versus a monetary union

	Flexible exchange rates	*Monetary union*
$w_{laggard1}/w_1$	decreasing	decreasing
$1/e_1$	~	~
$a_1/a_{laggard1}$	increasing	increasing
$w_{laggard1}/w_2$	increasing	decreasing
$1/e_1$	decreasing	constant
$a_2/a_{laggard1}$	increasing	increasing

The experiments above contain two regions that were falling behind, both belonging to country 1. In the upper panel of Table 6.1 the ratio in wages and labour productivity between a lagging region in country 1 to a 'normal' region (in the sense that it does not fall behind) in country 1 is shown. The wages of the laggard decrease relative to a region of their own country. In this case, the regional wage rate counteracts the difference in labour productivity.

The lower panel of Table 6.1 documents the components of the unit labour costs of a lagging region of country 1 compared to a region belonging to country 2. The lagging region shows an increasing technology gap toward the region from the other country. At first sight, it is surprising to see that the wages of the laggard increase instead of decrease. A decrease would have

---

[44] GDP per capita is in the model defined by Q/N. Note that $Q/N = Q/l * L/n = Q/L * l$. The employment rate in a Goodwin model is known to be subject to cycles (see Chapter 3). Therefore, GDP per capita is subject to cycling.

been expected, because the unit costs have to fall in order for this region to stay competitive. The increase in wages is caused by the fact that exchange rates act on a national level and therefore do not react to the increasing gap of one (or in this case two) regions. It happens to be the case that country 1 does not depreciate, it even appreciates. The high labour productivity of the non-falling behind regions in country 1 drives up the exchange rate. This has a negative effect on the lagging regions, because their regional wages have to adjust by an increase. In a way this points to the feature of Dutch disease: one 'activity' is driving up the exchange rate and decreasing competitiveness for the other 'activity' in the country. Only here several regions drive up the exchange rate for a few laggards.

The introduction of a monetary union has no important influence on this aspect of the behaviour of the model, because the exchange rate does not adapt when a few regions fall behind. Fixing the exchange rate, therefore, does not restrain the mechanism of adaptation. Even if the few laggards cause the average labour productivity of the first country to be much lower than the average labour productivity of the second country, the national exchange rate of the backward country is not affected. However, we only looked at the stylized situation in which just two regions in one country were falling behind. In the next section, we will examine the question of what would happen if more regions are falling behind.

3. SIMULATION RESULTS

3.1 Flexible exchange rates versus fixed exchange rates

In the recent literature, discussion has taken place about whether economic integration, more precisely a monetary union, will have overall positive or negative effects on the growth of the economies involved (Flam, 1992).

This section focuses on the introduction of irrevocably fixed exchange rates and the effects of this on growth. Some general characteristics of the simulations here, in comparison with the previous chapter, will be illustrated using the globe (because, in a sense, this provides the most interesting dynamics). Later on, a more complete analysis will be carried out for all three spheres.

The geographic space of the globe is distributed between two countries in such a way that each country comprises a different amount of regions. The first country contains 9 regions and is therefore labelled as small compared to the second country which consists of the remaining 23 regions. The analysis is initially limited to determining the effect of different exogenous rates of growth of the knowledge stock (ρ) across regions. In this experiment ρ was chosen from a range of decreasing sizes starting at [1.6, 2.0].

Figure 6.5: Frequency diagram of the coefficient of variation at the end of the run, disparity caused by the knowledge system in itself (shown in Chapter 5)

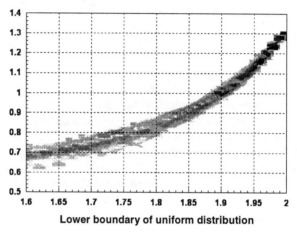

Lower boundary of uniform distribution

Figure 6.6: Frequency diagram of the coefficient of variation at the end of the run, disparity under flexible exchange rates

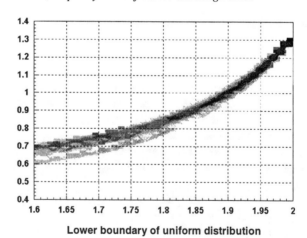

Lower boundary of uniform distribution

Figure 6.5 is reproduced from the previous chapter, where no countries were distinguished. The vertical axis shows the coefficient of variation of each run. The darker the pattern the higher the frequency. The horizontal axis indicates the lower boundary of the range out of which the exogenous rate of growth of the knowledge stock is randomly chosen (the upper boundary is set equal to 2). Figure 6.6 and 6.7 display the results for the same experiment for the multi-country model in this chapter under flexible and fixed exchange rates respectively. Figure 6.5 is virtually identical to Figure 6.6 and 6.7. The minor differences in shading are due to the random differences in runs. This indicates that the basic results of the model in this chapter are robust towards the results of the model in the former chapter, which did not implement countries.

Figure 6.7: Frequency diagram of the coefficient of variation at the end of the run, disparity under fixed exchange rates

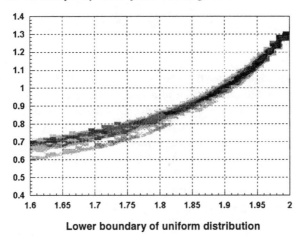

Lower boundary of uniform distribution

Another issue comes forward from comparing Figure 6.6 and 6.7. At first sight there seems to be no difference between the situation under flexible exchange rates and the introduction of a monetary union. However, if the exact values of the coefficient of variation are compared, we arrive at the result documented in Figure 6.8. The figure shows the coefficient of variation (the average over the last 100 periods) over the gaps in all regions for each run in two cases: flexible exchange rates and a monetary union. The exogenous rate of growth of the knowledge stock is set equal to 2; therefore every region has exactly the same initial parameters[45].

Figure 6.8: Overall disparity per run

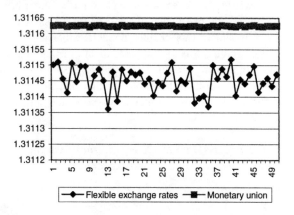

The figure highlights several things. First, the disparity under a monetary union is larger than under flexible exchange rates. This leads to the tentative conclusion that the introduction of a monetary union leads to an increase in the gaps of the regions. Second, the disparity under a monetary union shows less variability than the disparity under flexible exchange rates. A monetary union therefore leads also to a stabilization of the outcome. As can be seen in the figure, every experiment out of fifty generated this same distribution of gaps.

The question arises whether a monetary union will always cause a higher disparity across regions compared to the flexible exchange rate case. What influence do the parameters in the model have on the distribution of the gaps under a monetary union versus flexible exchange rates? To explore these questions we will address all geographic spaces starting with the lattice, followed by the column and the globe. Simulations were generated for several start values of the parameters and variables. At the start of each simulation all regions had exactly the same 'endowments', in the sense that

---

[45] Note that for this figure the experiments have used a learning capability equal to 4, whereas Figure 6.7 used a learning capability of 1. This is done, in order to envision the differences between a monetary union and flexible exchange rates more clearly. Further on in this chapter, we will explore in detail the effects of values of the learning capability on the differences in disparity caused by a fixed exchange rate system versus a system of flexible exchange rates. For Figure 6.8 it holds that ρ is set equal to 2 and the initial level of the knowledge stock is equal to 10 (as in Figures 6.5, 6.6 and 6.7).

each region has an equal learning capability, level of the knowledge stock, population and so on. (Appendix A shows the initial values of all parameters and variables). The geographic location is the only parameter that differs across regions. Across simulations, the parameters and variables were initially set at a different level. In each constellation, the coefficient of variation was determined in the case of flexible exchange rates and a monetary union. Figure 6.9 gives a visual impression of the results for the lattice of honeycombs. On the horizontal axis the value of the learning capability, which varied from 0.5 to 4.5 is denoted. The vertical axis shows the exogenous rate of growth of the knowledge stock that varied in the same interval. A grey cell indicates that the disparity under a monetary union was higher than under flexible exchange rates. The five different panels are made for five different values of the initial level of the knowledge stock.

Figure 6.9: Results for the lattice of honeycombs

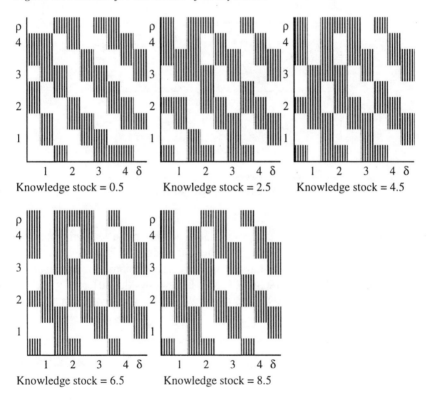

Several interesting phenomena are illustrated by this figure. First, a clear pattern is shown in the panels. There appear to be zones, which stretch from the upper left to the lower right. In each zone, either a monetary union or a system of flexible exchange rates causes more disparity across regions. The combination of learning capability and exogenous rate of growth of the knowledge stock therefore causes the disparity in the monetary union to be higher or lower than under flexible exchange rates. Second, as the knowledge stock is increased, some changes occur in the pattern, but these appear to be less systematic. This indicates that a change in the knowledge stock has some influence as well on whether a monetary union causes more disparity across regions than flexible exchange rates. We will analyse these general results in more detail.

Figure 6.10: Difference in disparity between a monetary union and flexible exchange rates, δ = 0.5, ρ =0.5

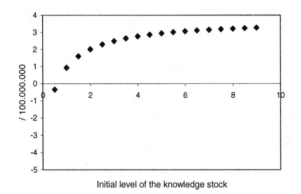

Initial level of the knowledge stock

Figure 6.10 focuses on one constellation in which the learning capability and the exogenous rate of growth of the knowledge stock are both set equal to 0.5[46]. This corresponds to the cell in the lower left corner of each panel in Figure 6.9. The horizontal axis of Figure 6.10 shows the different values for the initial level of the knowledge stock. When the knowledge stock is low,

---

[46] The same figure could be made with respect to a variation in the learning capability or the exogenous rate of growth of the knowledge stock. However, these constellations do not show any clear trends. This is already indicated by the complex pattern of grey and white in Figure [6.9]. Observing one column or row within a panel (meaning that the level of the knowledge stock is kept fixed as well as the learning capability or the exogenous rate of growth of the knowledge stock) we see that the colour changes frequently, indicating that the lowest disparity is generated by a monetary union and flexible exchange rates in turn.

for instance 0.5 or 1, the disparity that is generated by a monetary union is less than the disparity caused by a system of flexible exchange rates. As the initial level of the knowledge stock is increased, the monetary union shows an increasingly divergent effect compared to flexible exchange rates[47]. Finally, the curve becomes less steep and the effect stabilizes. A similar trend is also found if we examine other combinations of the learning capability with the exogenous rate of growth of the knowledge stock as in Figure 6.11.

Figure 6.11: Difference in disparity between a monetary union and flexible exchange rates, $\delta = 1$, $\rho = 1$

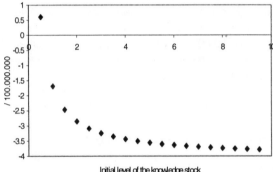

Note that the pattern in Figure 6.8 may also be reversed, that is, a monetary union leading to higher disparity between runs. Figure 6.11 illustrates this by showing a case in which the parameter constellation has this effect.

Figure 6.9 also shows several cells that do not change colour as the knowledge stock is increased. In these cells, an upward or downward trend in terms of the Figures 6.10 and 6.11 occurs as well. In general, it is the case that if the knowledge stock has reached a relatively high value (8.5), the cells will not change colour any more. The situation is now stable in that either the monetary union or the flexible exchange rates case shows the largest disparity.

This overall result emphasizes that under certain combinations of the learning capability and the exogenous rate of growth of the knowledge stock more disparity might occur as a result of the introduction of a monetary

---

[47] The difference is quite small in absolute terms; however, a clear difference is present. Note that the coefficient of variation over the gaps in labour productivity is taken, in which the gap is defined by a logarithmic function, which suppresses high values.

union. This contradicts the general belief that the introduction of a monetary union will generate convergence across the participating countries/regions.

More precisely, the results indicate that both parameters (the learning capability, δ, and the exogenous rate of growth of the knowledge stock, ρ) *and* a variable (the level of the knowledge stock at the start of the simulation) all have an influence on whether a monetary union induces a lower or higher disparity across regions than flexible exchange rates. The influence of the initial level of the knowledge stock becomes marginal as it reaches a high value. This is based on Figure 6.9 in which not many changes in colour take place any more once the knowledge stock has a value of 8.5 and higher. However, the influence of δ and ρ is much higher. An enlargement of the learning capability (keeping ρ and the initial level of the knowledge stock equal) will lead to several switches in colour in Figure 6.9. This indicates that a small change in the learning capability induces a new situation in which either a monetary union or flexible exchange rates cause the highest disparity across regions. The exogenous rate of growth of the knowledge stock has a less strong impact. As ρ is increased (all other things being equal) there appear large intervals in which a monetary union generates a larger disparity across regions than flexible exchange rates, and vice versa. This might lead to the conclusion that it is easier to use the exogenous rate of growth of the knowledge stock as a policy instrument (for example by increasing the amount of R&D) than to influence the learning capability of all regions. Influencing the learning capability might lead to overshooting the objective that the introduction of a monetary union leads to less disparity than would be the case if flexible exchange rates were maintained.

Until now attention has been focused on one aspect, namely under which conditions a monetary union induces a lower or higher disparity than flexible exchange rates. Figures 6.10 and 6.11 indicated that the *difference* between the disparity generated by the two stages of integration increases as the initial level of the knowledge stock is increased. However, it is also worth studying the absolute effect of the initial level of the knowledge stock on disparity in general, under a monetary union as well as under flexible exchange rates. The disparity under a monetary union and flexible exchange rates could increase as a result of an increase in the initial level of the knowledge stock; however, the *difference* between the two could become smaller. The objective would then be to find the situation in which disparity across regions is minimal.

Observing the several combinations of δ and ρ and focusing on the effect on disparity under a monetary union and flexible exchange rates as the initial level of the knowledge stock is increased for all regions, the following result is obtained. Under flexible exchange rates as well as under a monetary union the disparity across regions decreases as the initial level of the knowledge stock is increased. This decrease occurs at a diminishing rate, leading to the conclusion that an overall increase in the knowledge stock ameliorates the situation of the economy in that disparity across regions is decreased.

Figure 6.12: Results for the column

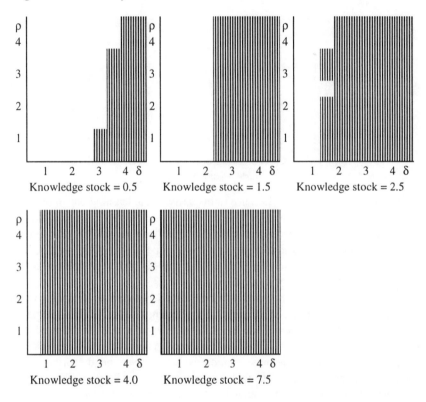

Figure 6.12 shows the results for the column. The patterns are quite different from those for the lattice. Starting with a knowledge stock of 0.5 (for all regions) two distinct areas emerge. The grey area shows the parameter values for which the coefficient of variation of the monetary union is higher than for the system of flexible exchange rates. The opposite is the case for the white area.

This figure indicates that, as the level of the knowledge stock is increased, the grey area is enlarged, until finally the parameters no longer have an influence on the direction of the difference. For each combination of δ and ρ, a monetary union causes a larger disparity than a system of flexible exchange rates.

Figure 6.13: Difference in disparity between a monetary union and flexible exchange rates, δ = 1, ρ = 1

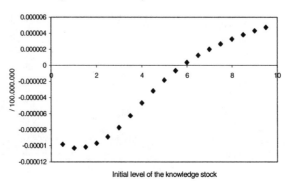

Figure 6.13 shows the difference in disparity as the learning capability and the exogenous rate of growth of the knowledge stock are both set equal to 0.5 and the knowledge stock is gradually increased from 0.5 to 9.5. The figure clearly shows that the knowledge stock has a value between 5.5 and 6 as the disparity caused by a monetary union starts to be higher compared to the disparity under a system of flexible exchange rates.

A similar pattern to the one described above is found as a result of the simulations with the globe (Figure 5.14). Again, a clear division appears between the grey and the white area. As the knowledge stock is enlarged, the grey area becomes larger. Thus, we find more constellations in which the disparity caused by a monetary union is larger than the disparity under flexible exchange rates. Note that the sequence in which the grey area is enlarged is different from the sequence found for the column. Whereas in the case of the column the white area is reduced from right to left, here we see that from the point that the knowledge stock is equal to 4.5 a grey area emerges at the left-hand side of the panel, reducing the white area from left to right.

When the cell closest to the origin (δ = 0.5, ρ = 0.5) is explored in further detail, we come across similar results as shown in the case of the column. The difference in disparity between a monetary union and flexible exchange rates increases as the knowledge stock is increased (see Figure 6.15). In both situations, a monetary union and a system of flexible exchange rates, the disparity across regions increases as the knowledge stock is increased. As shown in Figure 6.14, a variation in ρ does not have a large impact on disparity. This is indicated by the fact that a switch in colour rarely occurs as ρ is increased. A variation in δ, however, does have an impact on disparity.

Figure 6.14: Results for the globe

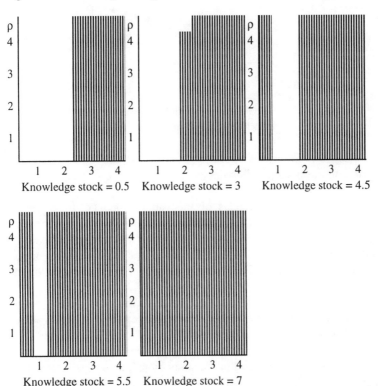

This section illustrates what effects different conditions (constellations of parameters like the learning capability and the exogenous rate of growth of the knowledge stock) have on the disparity in the gaps of the knowledge stock across regions. These conditions are explored in two different stages of integration, namely a monetary union and a system of flexible exchange rates. The choice of the geographical sphere has a large impact on the results. The lattice of honeycombs might be the most realistic sphere to compare with the European Union. In this sphere, we see that specific combinations of the learning capability and the exogenous rate of growth of the knowledge stock lead to less disparity across regions in the case of a monetary union, but other combinations show an adverse effect.

Figure 6.15: Difference in disparity between a monetary union and flexible exchange rates, $\delta = 0.5$, $\rho = 0.5$

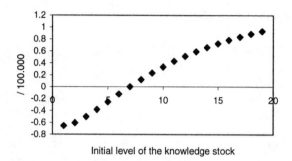

Initial level of the knowledge stock

3.2 Barriers to knowledge spillovers

The existence of national systems of innovation stimulates inter-country regional interaction rather than cross-border relationships. The experiments in this section aim to explore the effect of barriers to knowledge spillovers. In this section a barrier to knowledge spillovers across countries is introduced by reducing the spillovers that cross the border between the countries by one half.

Various experiments are carried out, which differ with respect to the geographical sphere that is used and the parameter or variable that is varied. Figure 6.16 shows the results based on the lattice of honeycombs. The coefficient of variation at the start of the simulation is plotted against the coefficient of variation at the end of the simulation. Two things emerge from this figure. First, as the initial coefficient of variation has a value between 0.4 and 0.7 the observations are quite dispersed. This points to a falling behind of regions within the leading country. Second, at the right-hand side of Figure 6.16, a higher coefficient of variation appears than at the left-hand side. Thus, the final disparity across gaps on the right is high when the initial disparity across knowledge stocks was relatively high as well. When we move from right to left in the figure, the coefficient of variation at the start of the simulation decreases. Apparently, this leads to a lower disparity at the end of the simulation. We will come back to both effects later on.

The two panels in Figure 6.17 show the effect of a variation in the learning capability and the exogenous rate of growth of the knowledge stock, respectively. Both parameters are drawn from a uniform distribution of decreasing size, where, as before, the upper boundary is fixed and the lower boundary is shifted. The horizontal axis in each panel in Figure 6.17 shows the lower boundary of this range. The upper boundary was set equal to 2 throughout the simulations[48]. The vertical axis shows the frequency of the coefficient of variation of the gaps.

Figure 6.16: The effect of barriers to knowledge spillovers on the lattice of honeycombs (coefficient of variation at the start of the simulation is plotted against the coefficient of variation at the end of the simulation)

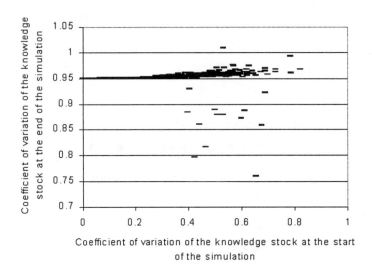

Note that in both panels the right-most coefficient of variation is lower than in previous experiments (Section 3.1). This is partly due to the fact that by introducing barriers to cross border spillovers, the total spillover that occurs in the model is reduced[49]. On the other hand, this lower coefficient of

---

[48] Appendix A of this chapter shows the values of all parameters and variables in the model. Different from these values are the values for δ, ρ and the initial level of the knowledge stock, as these are not varied in an experiment (and are therefore equal across regions). In this case δ and ρ are both set equal to 1. As the initial level of the knowledge stock is not subject to variation it is set equal to 10.

[49] For the same reason, the regions are allocated to countries in a way that each country comprises a similar amount of regions. That is, for the lattice, country 1 consists of 10 and country 2 of 9 regions. The column allocates 10 regions to country 1 and 11 to country 2. For the globe, both countries have an equal amount of regions, namely 16.

variation is also partly generated by the specific characteristics of this experiment, which will become clear in the remainder of this section.

Figure 6.17: Panel 1: Frequency diagram of the coefficient of variation at the end of the run; a variation in the learning capability

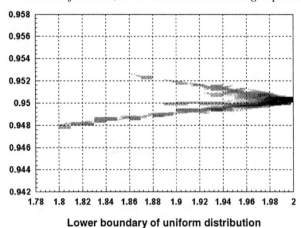

Lower boundary of uniform distribution

Panel 2: Frequency diagram of the coefficient of variation at the end of the run; a variation in the exogenous growth of knowledge generation

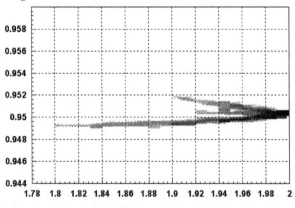

Lower boundary of uniform distribution

The first panel of Figure 6.17 shows the results for a variation in the learning capability. A comet-shape appears, in which 'the comet' (the dark spot at the right of the figure) leaves two clear trails: a long one coming from the lower left and a shorter trail originating from the upper left. This indicates that an increase in initial disparity across regions induces two effects. The upper trail suggests higher disparity; however, a stronger effect originates from the lower trail, which suggests smaller disparity across regions. The more unequal regions are in terms of their learning capability, the more differences in disparity exist across runs.

A similar comet-shape appears when we observe the results for a variation in the exogenous rate of growth of the knowledge stock (Figure 6.17, Panel 2). Again, there appear two trails of which the lower one is longer. Based on this observation, a variation in the exogenous rate of growth of the knowledge stock seems to have the same influence on the behaviour of the model than a variation in the learning capability.

When we observe both panels of Figure 6.17, we see that the dark spot at the right-hand side of the figure (the coefficient of variation when there are no differences across regions in parameter values or variable levels at the start of the simulation) has the same value. This value is identical to the one at the left-most side in Figure 6.16. It is interesting to observe the distribution of the gaps across regions at this point. Figure 6.18 reveals the pattern in the gaps at this parameter constellation. The number within each honeycomb indicates the size of the gap of the region toward the leader region[50]. The thick line demarcates the border between the two countries.

The pattern shows strong inter-country variation, rather than interregional variation. The origins for this pattern are found in the first periods of the run. The second country comprises the region that on a world level has the most favourable geographic location, the central region. This simple fact causes the second country to become the leader in the end. The centrally located region (in the world) will receive most spillovers in the first periods of the run, only because of its central position. At the same time the regions of country one, bordering this central region, are faced by a large disadvantage of the border. Their spillovers from the advanced country two are reduced by one half. This process is reinforced as the simulation time passes.

A second observation is that in the second country the leader region is located in the most favourable geographic position (the central location) within the country. The world-leader region is therefore not the 'overall' central region in the world. The other regions within country two show gaps which are (line-) symmetrically distributed around the leader region. Thus, within country two the 'usual' polarization takes place, in the sense that the

---

[50] Note that these are average values over the last 100 periods in a run.

regions that are geographically close to the central region display the lowest gaps.

Figure 6.18: The distribution of the gaps over two countries on the lattice

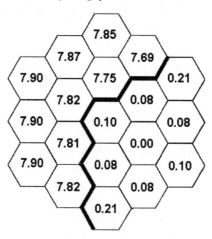

What is the specific effect of introducing knowledge barriers to this model? This question can be analysed by comparing these results to the results found in Chapter 5. With respect to the variation in the knowledge stocks of the regions, it is useful to compare Figure 6.16 with Figure 5.4.

The right side of Figure 6.16 displays many observations with a coefficient of variation ranging from nearly 0.95 up to almost 0.98. The broadness of the range indicates that many runs have a similar, though slightly different, coefficient of variation. The differences in disparity within this small range are due to the 'normal' variation between runs within one interval.

The figure displays a few observations with a coefficient of variation of about 0.875. This is the effect of regions within the second country (the leader) falling behind. Falling behind in this experiment is much less compared to the strong presence in the case of no barriers to knowledge spillovers. Falling behind in Figure 6.16 leads to less final disparity in this case, contrary to the case of no barriers to knowledge spillovers in which falling behind induced a higher disparity at the end of the simulation. This is due to the existence of two countries. In this case, the regions within the first country experience a large gap towards the leader region, which is located in the second country (see Figure 6.18). When a region from within country 2 experiences falling behind (due to unfavourable low initial values of its knowledge stock), this induces the overall disparity to decline. Since only a small number of runs is subject to falling behind, we can conclude that under barriers to knowledge spillovers, falling behind has less of an impact on the disparity than before.

Another point originates from Figure 6.16. At the right-hand side, the coefficient of variation is slightly higher than on the left, while this effect is absent from Figure 5.4. This phenomenon finds its origin in the barriers to knowledge spillovers between the countries. Because the first country receives few spillovers due to the barriers to cross-border spillovers, the equilibrium gap (towards every individual region from this country) continues to grow during the transitory dynamics. At a high initial coefficient of variation (right-hand side of the figure), large initial differences between regions are present. Apparently, this causes a relatively high variety of equilibrium gaps across regions (of the first country) within a run. Therefore, the overall disparity is higher than in the case where initial differences across regions are smaller (left-hand side of the figure).

Figure 6.19: The effect of barriers to knowledge spillovers on the column; (coefficient of variation at the start of the simulation is plotted against the coefficient of variation at the end of the simulation)

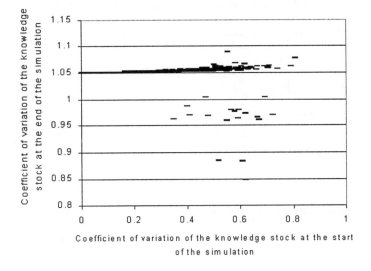

With respect to a variation in one of the parameters (learning capability or exogenous rate of growth of the knowledge stock) both panels in Figure 5.17 show clear trails, which were absent before in the corresponding figures in Chapter 5 (Figures 5.12 and 5.15). This means that two states appear most often as the initial differences across regions increase with respect to one of the two parameters. In one state the disparity is larger than in the distribution shown by Figure 6.18, in the other state the disparity in the gaps across regions is smaller.

Figure 6.19 shows the results for the column, concerning an initial variation in the knowledge stock across regions. Compared to the lattice we observe only little difference in the shape of the pattern. This is different when a variation in the learning capability is considered (Figure 6.20, Panel 1). Again the comet-shape appears, leaving two trails. However, the location of the trails differs from what is observed in the case of the lattice. Here, a high trail with a downward slope is the strongest. Next to this trail, there is a vague indication of a second trail with a horizontal slope. However, this second trail is less strong. This indicates that an increase in the initial differences across regions with respect to their initial learning capability generally leads to more disparity in the case of knowledge barriers. This is contrary to the result we found before (Chapter 5), when an increase in initial differences led to a decrease in disparity (Figure 5.13).

Figure 6.20: Panel 1: Frequency diagram of the coefficient of variation at the end of the run; a variation in the learning capability

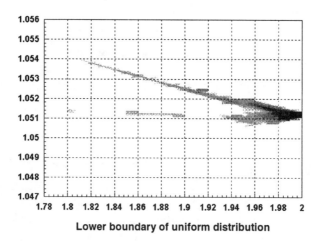

Lower boundary of uniform distribution

The second panel in Figure 6.20 depicts the influence of a variation in the exogenous rate of growth of the knowledge stock under barriers to knowledge spillovers. It shows a pattern in which two trails occur. The high downward sloping trail is the strongest. Again, a clear difference appears as compared with the former results. Before, we found a clear upward trend

(Figure 5.17, Panel 2). Here this trend is also present, but a stronger downward-sloping trend accompanies it.

Panel 2: Frequency diagram of the coefficient of variation at the end of the run; a variation in the exogenous growth of knowledge generation

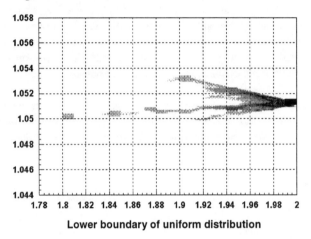

Lower boundary of uniform distribution

Figure 6.21: The distribution of the gaps over two countries on the column

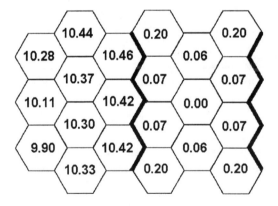

The distribution of the gaps without initial differences across regions looks as displayed in Figure 6.21. The same phenomenon occurs as before with the lattice. One of the countries shows relatively large gaps (country 1), while the other shows relatively small gaps (country 2). Moreover, regions with a relatively small gap in country 2 (gaps of 0.06 and 0.07) surround the world-leader region. The second order neighbours (within country 2) of the leader display a gap of 0.20. Thus, the second country displays a pattern of polarization around the centrally located region, in the sense that at larger geographical distance from the leader region the gaps become larger.

This is clearly distinct from the situation without barriers to knowledge spillovers in which overall polarization occurred. From this, we can conclude that barriers to knowledge spillovers lead to differences between countries. A backward country emerges, in which all the regions have a large gap towards the world-leader region. Within the leader country, polarization takes place guided by geographic distances as we have seen before.

Figure 6.22: The effect of barriers to knowledge spillovers on the globe; (coefficient of variation at the start of the simulation is plotted against the coefficient of variation at the end of the simulation)

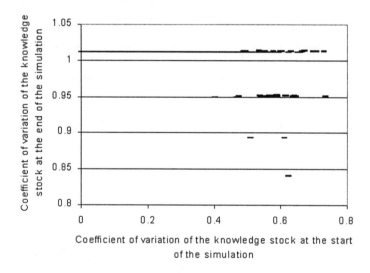

The sphere used in the last set of simulations is the globe. Figure 6.22 displays the results for a variation in the knowledge stock. A variation in the initial stock of knowledge across regions leads to a disparity in gaps across regions as displayed in Figure 6.22. Whereas the final disparity of 1.0117 is seen to result independently of the initial disparity across regions, there are occasions when a lower final coefficient of variation occurs. Similar to the experiment for the lattice of honeycombs this is due to falling behind within the leader country.

Figure 6.23: Panel 1: Frequency diagram of the coefficient of variation at the end of the run; a variation in the learning capability

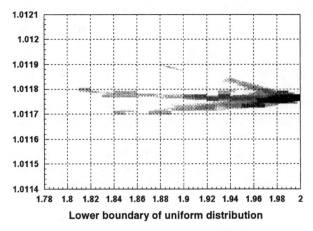

Panel 2: Frequency diagram of the coefficient of variation at the end of the run; a variation in the exogenous growth of knowledge generation

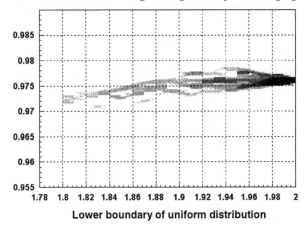

Panel 1 of Figure 6.23 shows the disparity in each run for a variation in the learning capability. A comet-shape occurs, indicating that an increase in initial disparity across regions induces not only less disparity across regions at the end of the simulation but could also cause more disparity. The more unequal regions are in terms of their exogenous rate of growth of the knowledge stock, the more differences in disparity exist across runs.

However, there seem to be (three) different paths along which the coefficient of variation moves (three trails). One trail is moving upward from the black cell towards the upper left. A second path stretches out in a slightly downward direction (from right to left). The third trail is horizontal. Panel 2 shows the results for a variation in the learning capability. Again, a comet-shape appears; however, no separate trails are distinguished.

In general, the figures for this geographical sphere show similar trends as for the other spheres, although the amount, direction and clarity of the trails (for an initial random variation in δ or ρ) differs somewhat.

Summarizing, what is the effect of the introduction of barriers to knowledge spillovers on the model in this sphere? Panels 1 and 2 of Figure 6.23 are quite distinct from the situation in which no barriers to spillovers occur. The shape of the comet-trail in the former experiments looked like an upward-sloping curve, indicating that disparity was low at large intervals. Figure 6.23 shows quite a large variety in disparity at large intervals. The coefficient of variation is not necessarily below the level of the case in which all regions are completely similar with respect to ρ, δ and the initial level of the knowledge stock. Therefore, barriers to knowledge spillovers induce more disparity across runs when the regions are more different initially.

Figure 6.24: The distribution of the gaps over two countries on the globe

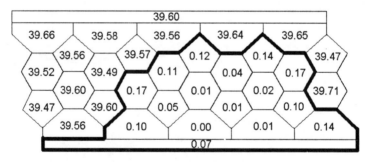

The distribution connected to the situation in which regions have the same initial values is shown by Figure 6.24[51, 52].

---

[51] It might strike as remarkable that Panel 2 shows a lower final coefficient of variation than in Panel 1. This is due to the fact that learning capability is set equal to 2 in this experiment, while it was set equal to 1 in the first set of simulations.

[52] Note that the geographic structure of country 2 is asymmetrical. Therefore, it is less easy to see that the leader region is centrally located within country 2. In Appendix B, the same experiment has been executed for a different, symmetric geographic structure for both countries. The results with respect to disparity (for all ranges) are similar. The only advantage of a symmetric

This set of experiments sheds light on the effect of barriers to knowledge spillovers on the model. A striking result is that a clear difference in the average gap between two countries occurs. In one country, all regions will tend to an equilibrium in which their gap toward the leader region (located in the other country) is very large. The country containing the leader region shows polarization. This result indicates that the 'adverse' effect of variety in learning capability and exogenous rate of growth of the knowledge stock, as was demonstrated in Chapter 5, only holds within a country.

4. SUMMARY AND CONCLUSIONS

This chapter developed a multi-country model, in which interregional knowledge spillovers determine the growth of regions. By simulations we examined the effect of parameters such as the learning capability and the exogenous rate of growth of the knowledge stock on disparity in different situations. First, the effect of barriers to trade was investigated by comparing two different stages of integration. A fixed exchange rate system versus a system of flexible exchange rates was examined, resulting in conditions (constellations of parameters) under which fixed exchange rates (compared to flexible exchange rates) generate less disparity across regions. However, depending on the parameter values, fixed exchange rates may also generate more disparity, leading to the conclusion that the effect of monetary integration is ambiguous.

Second, attention was paid to barriers to knowledge spillovers in the sense that cross-border knowledge flows are hampered compared to inter-country flows. This experiment leads to the result that reduced cross-border flows have a significant implication when regions are initially unequal with respect to the exogenous rate of growth of the knowledge stock or the learning capability. In these cases, the resulting trends in overall disparity are quite different from the trends established in a situation of no barriers to knowledge spillovers[53].

The most important result from this last experiment is that a difference between countries appears in the resulting pattern of per capita gaps. One of the two countries contains the leader region and this region is located centrally within this country. All other regions of the leader country are grouped in a hierarchical pattern around the central region. The other country

---

geographic structure is that it enables us to see immediately the polarization around the central region of the leader country.

[53] This holds especially for the column and the globe.

contains regions that have a large gap towards the world-leader region. This indicates that, with limited cross-border spillovers, the 'adverse' effect of variety in learning capability and exogenous rate of growth of the knowledge stock, as was demonstrated in Chapter 5, only holds within a country.

APPENDIX A: DEFAULT LEVELS OF THE VARIABLES AND VALUES OF THE PARAMETERS

Time simulated	1000
Knowledge stock	2-10*
Exogenous rate of growth of the knowledge stock	0.5-2*
Learning capability	0.5-2*
mu	1
beta	0.005
alpha	0.005
lambda (Verdoorn parameter)	0.1
dzeta	1
c	3
d	1
m	0.8
n	1
eta	0.008
epsilon	0.01
Exchange rate country 1 (exchange rate country two = 1)	1.14

Notes: The variable or parameter is set equal for all regions to the lower boundary of this interval and then increases per run with step 0.5 to the higher boundary.

APPENDIX B: THE EFFECTS OF BARRIERS TO KNOWLEDGE SPILLOVERS FOR A GLOBE CONTAINING TWO SYMMETRIC COUNTRIES

Figure 6.25: Two countries on a globe

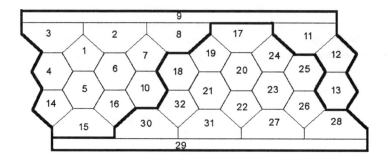

Figure 6.25 presents a geographic structure of the globe that is different from that in Appendix B of Chapter 5. A thick line demarcates a country. Regions 10 and 17 switched places in order to make the two countries used in this chapter symmetrical.

Figure 6.26: The gaps for the experiment in Section 3.2

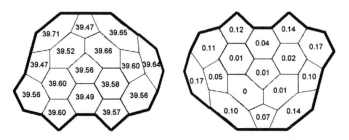

Figure 6.27: The gaps for the alternative geographic structure

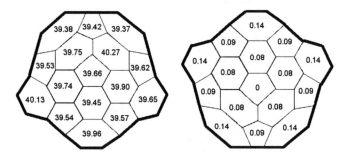

Figure 6.26 displays the gaps of the experiment in Section 3.2. The figure shows the top-view and bottom-view of the globe, looking at country 1 and 2 respectively. The gaps in both countries induced by the symmetric geographical pattern are shown in Figure 6.27. Comparing the shapes of the countries in Figure 6.26 with Figure 6.27 clearly illustrates the difference with respect to symmetry. Although in Figure 6.26 the leader is located in the geographically most favourable position within country 2, this is less obvious from the figure. Figure 6.27, however, clearly shows that within country 2 a polarization (hierarchical pattern) around the central region is present. The pattern of gaps for country 1 gives no indication of polarization.

7. GDP per Capita Gaps, the Situation for European Regions

The aim of this (and the next) chapter is to relate the model developed in Chapters 4 and 6 to the present situation in Europe. In these chapters a technology gap model was developed. Knowledge spillovers were assumed to take place on the basis of the specific characteristics of a region, among others its geographic location and its technological distance from other regions. This diffusion of knowledge was assumed to be a gradual process. Over time, part of the knowledge of each region spilled over to other regions.

The gradual diffusion of knowledge over time resulted in certain equilibrium patterns in the distribution of knowledge, and hence production over regions. These equilibrium patterns show situations in which GDP per capita gaps are (roughly) constant, but unequally distributed over space. Section 1 of this chapter will explore European regional data in order to investigate to what extent the empirically observed patterns resemble those generated by the model.

In the model of Chapters 4 and 6 the accumulation of knowledge in each region is determined by the received spillovers, the learning capability and the exogenous rate of growth of the knowledge stock. Differences across regions in the exogenous rate of growth of the knowledge stock and the learning capability are important for the equilibrium distribution of per capita gaps. Section 2 will explore the geographic distribution of these parameters across Europe by using R&D data as an indicator.

In order to be able to influence the distribution of GDP per capita gaps for policy goals, it is important to determine which variables are related to the learning capability and the exogenous rate of growth of the knowledge stock. By means of regressions, Section 3 will determine whether variables such as population density and higher education R&D are correlated to the R&D intensity of a region.

Finally, Section 4 will determine the long-run distribution of the learning capability and the exogenous rate of growth of the knowledge stock by means of transition matrices. This will give insight into the question whether differences across regions in learning capability and exogenous rate of growth of the knowledge stock persist over time.

Figure 7.1: GDP per capita across European regions

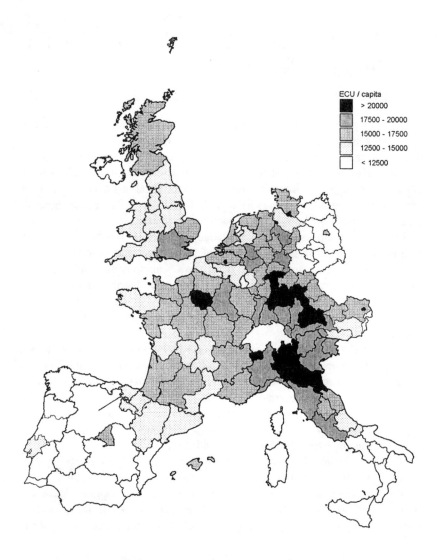

Source: EPO, EUROSTAT

1. THE GEOGRAPHIC DISTRIBUTION OF GDP PER CAPITA ACROSS EUROPEAN REGIONS

Throughout this and the next chapter, the Nomenclature des Unités Territoriales Statistiques (NUTS) is used for defining regions[54]. Although the NUTS classification is often the only one for which consistent data are available, using this classification has certain known disadvantages. The classification reflects administrative units which differ in size (Molle, 1980). Here, the NUTS level for each country was chosen such that differences in size across regions are largely compensated. Furthermore, a region defined by administrative boundaries does not necessarily reflect the area that would be enclosed by economic boundaries reflecting regions with similar economic characteristics (Richardson, 1978a and b). Moreover, such an administrative classification cannot circumvent the fact that regions vary in administrative functions between countries (Molle, 1980). However, a classification in administrative units might be considered an important advantage while studying the policy implications of the analysis.

Within Europe, GDP per capita (in 1992) is distributed as shown in Figure 7.1. A dark colour indicates a high GDP per capita. The figure illustrates that the geographic distribution of GDP per capita is concentrated to a large degree. Areas with the highest GDP per capita are located in the south of Germany and the north of Italy. Each of these regions has a GDP per capita (in Purchasing Power Standard) of 20000 ECU per inhabitant or more.

The impression given by the figure is that regions with a high GDP per capita are surrounded by regions with a similar level of GDP per capita, that is, clustering occurs. In order to investigate this further, in other words, to quantify the degree to which the value of a variable in one region is spatially correlated to the value in neighbouring regions, a concept well known in geography is used. This concept, called spatial autocorrelation (Cliff and Ord, 1973), enables us to identify a significant non-random arrangement in an area pattern of a certain variable. In Figure 7.2 an example is given of positive and negative spatial autocorrelation.

---

[54] See Appendix A for the NUTS classification used in this chapter and Appendix D for the geographic location of each NUTS region.

Figure 7.2: Spatial patterns, inspired by McGrew and Monroe (1993)

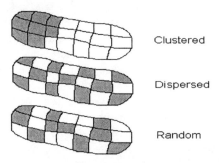

Clustered

Dispersed

Random

The basic property of spatially autocorrelated data is that the values are distributed non-randomly (or are interdependent) over space. The clustered pattern exhibits positive spatial autocorrelation, with neighbouring locations having similar values. The dispersed pattern has negative autocorrelation, with nearby locations having dissimilar values. Random area patterns have no spatial autocorrelation (McGrew and Monroe, 1993).

Spatial autocorrelation can be measured using the coefficient of Moran. This coefficient is defined in the following way:

$$I = \left(\frac{n}{W}\right)\frac{\sum_{i=1}^{n}\sum_{\substack{j=1\\i\neq j}}^{n}\left(w_{ij}z_{i}z_{j}\right)}{\sum_{i}^{n}z_{i}^{2}}, \tag{7.1}$$

where $z_i = x_i - x$ (x_i is the value of the variable under consideration in region i, x denotes the average value of the variable over all regions) and

$$W = \sum_{\substack{i=1\\i\neq j}}^{n}\sum_{j=1}^{n}w_{ij}$$

(see Cliff and Ord, 1973). Here n points to the total number of regions and w_{ij} denotes the element on the ith row and jth column of the matrix of n times n weights. The n times n matrix of weights is crucial to this statistic. In this matrix, a neighbouring region (in the sense that both regions share one border) is assigned a weight of 1 ($w_{ij} = 1$). Regions that do not share a border but are still closely located to region 1 are given a weight by using the concept of nearest neighbours (see Chapter 5 for an explanation of this concept)[55].

---

[55] In the calculation of the coefficient of Moran, we only took into account neighbours up to the fourth order, since beyond that distance we do not expect any spillovers due to geographic proximity.

The pattern of GDP per capita generated by the model in Chapters 4 and 6 suggests positive spatial autocorrelation. It was shown that in the absence of differences between regions in terms of knowledge generation or learning capability, centrally located regions achieve high GDP per capita levels, with 'spheres' of gradually less rich regions around them. Differences in knowledge generation or learning capability (assumed to be random in the theoretical set-up) may lead to (small) distortions of this spatial pattern, but never to the extent that no spatial autocorrelation seems to be present. We will now proceed to investigate whether such positive spatial autocorrelation exists for the case of European regions in the early 1990s.

Table 7.1 shows that significant clustering occurs. Between countries, large differences in the degree of spatial autocorrelation exist. Figure 7.3 shows the distribution of GDP per capita across French, Spanish, German, Italian and British regions. The coefficient of Moran in Table 7.1 indicates that Spain has the highest degree of clustering followed by Italy and France. Note that Germany displays the lowest coefficient of Moran, while that might not directly appear from the figure. The low degree of clustering is caused by the fact that German regions show large extremes with respect to GDP per capita. The poorest region (located in former East-Germany) has a GDP per capita below 6000 Ecu, while the wealthiest region (Hamburg) has a GDP per capita larger than 30000 Ecu. In Figure 7.3, this large spectrum is represented by the large categories in shading. Therefore, clustering appears to be present.

These results, by and large, seem to confirm the presence of spatial autocorrelation of GDP per capita across Europe.

Table 7.1: Clustering within Europe

	Coefficient of Moran	*(t-value)*
Europe[a]	0.3204[c]	3.7435
France[b]	0.1662[c]	1.7332
Spain[b]	0.4536[c]	3.3653
United Kingdom[b]	0.1248	1.1417
Italy[a]	0.6691[c]	3.3172
Germany[a]	0.0221	0.3260

Notes: [a] NUTS 2
    [b] NUTS 3
    [c] significant at the 5% level

Figure 7.3: The distribution of GDP per capita across French, Spanish, German, Italian and British regions

Panel 1: France

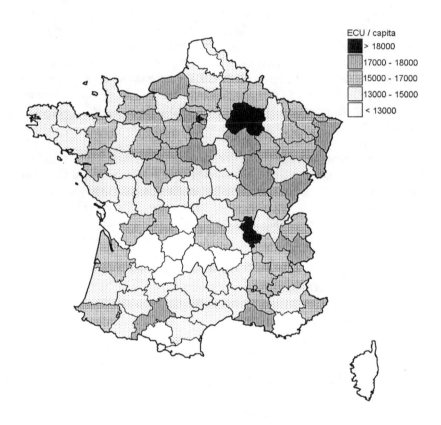

Source: EUROSTAT

Panel 2: Spain

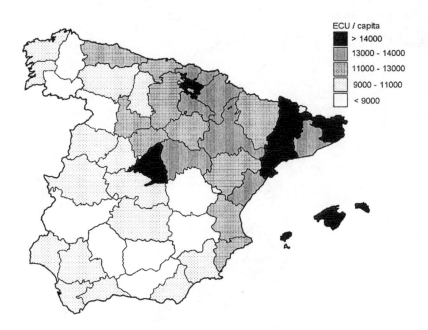

Source: EUROSTAT

Panel 3: Germany

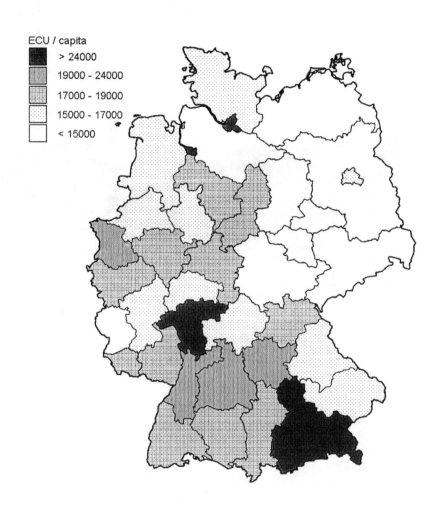

Source: EUROSTAT

Panel 4: Italy

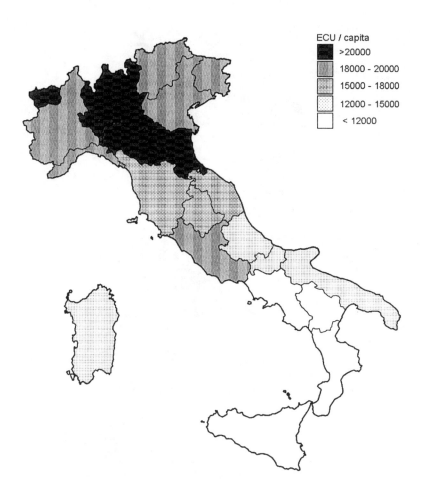

Source: EUROSTAT

Panel 5: United Kingdom

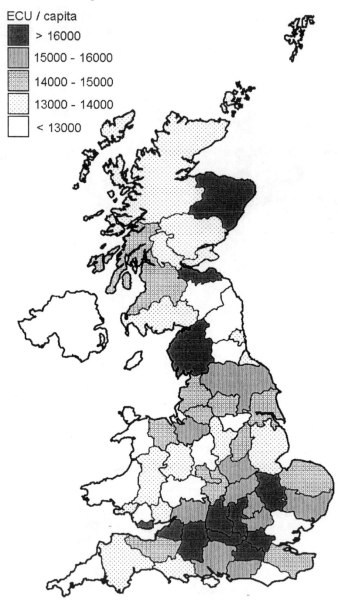

2. THE GEOGRAPHIC DISTRIBUTION OF R&D IN EUROPE

The model in Chapters 4 and 6 states, in general terms, that differences in the exogenous rate of growth of the knowledge stock and the learning capability are very important for determining the distribution of GDP per capita gaps. These two parameters cannot be measured directly by the available data. However, R&D expenditures can be used as an indicator. The link between the exogenous rate of growth of the knowledge stock and R&D is quite straightforward: R&D investments enhance the growth of the knowledge stock. The link between R&D and the learning capability was suggested by Cohen and Levinthal (1989).

They argue that firms engage in R&D not only to pursue new product and process innovations, but also to increase their general knowledge, which makes them capable of assimilating knowledge spillovers from outside the firm. This external knowledge may induce the firm to generate innovations, which would not have been possible if the firm did not have the capability to implement the knowledge spillovers. This second reason reflects the link between R&D and learning capability.

Note that the model in Chapters 4 and 6 did not assume any spatial correlation in terms of knowledge generation or learning capability. Differences in these parameters were assumed to be purely random. Obviously, this was a simplifying assumption made mainly for convenience. In reality, differences in these parameters may well be systematic. What matters here, however, is only whether or not such differences exist, and how large they are. (The next section will explore some possible explaining factors). Therefore, a different indicator than the coefficient of Moran will be used.

An index that can be used to indicate whether a variable is distributed evenly over regions is the Herfindahl index (defined as $\Sigma^{n}_{i=1} S_i^2$, where S_i denotes the share of the variable of region i in the total of the variable of the country and n is the number of regions in a country). Since the extreme values of this index are dependent on the number of regions in a country, the Herfindahl index used in this chapter is rescaled to bring it within the interval [0,1] for every country[56]. Mathematically, this operation can be rewritten into the following equation:

---

[56] The *ln* function is used to give the index a gradual increase (decline) when the degree of concentration gradually becomes higher (lower). See Appendix C for the mathematical operations imposed on the original Herfindahl index.

$$HF = 1 + \frac{\ln \sum_{i=1}^{n} S_i^2}{\ln n},$$

(7.2)

where *HF* denotes the adjusted Herfindahl index[57]. The higher the value of this index, the higher the geographical concentration in a certain region.

Different R&D data is used, namely data on high technology employment (HTE), R&D expenditures and R&D personnel. All the empirical operations in this chapter were conducted using the EUROSTAT REGIO database[58].

Table 7.2 shows the value of the Herfindahl index, as defined in Equation (7.2), in 1991 for nine different variables. A few points emerge from the table. A first point is that looking at the different variables for one country, the Herfindahl index for business enterprise R&D is considerably higher than the Herfindahl index for GDP or the working population. This is true for all countries. This points to the fact that R&D performed by business enterprise is not distributed evenly across regions. In fact, it is concentrated geographically to a larger extent than would be expected on the basis of the geographical concentration of GDP or the working population.

A second point that emerges clearly from the table is that the Herfindahl index for HTE is much lower than the indexes for both R&D indicators of business enterprise. This might be due to the fact that much R&D is performed in headquarters, therefore R&D indicators show a higher geographical concentration than HTE. As can be seen from Table 7.2, HTE is still more concentrated than the working population for most countries, which is an indication of the existence of technology gaps.

Third, in comparing business R&D with higher education R&D, the former is far more geographically concentrated for most countries. This is true for the R&D expenditure data as well as for the R&D employee data. This could be due to the fact that in determining the distribution of higher education across a country, a large role is played by government. In most cases the government of a country will pursue an equal distribution of, for example, universities across the country, which would account for a somewhat lower Herfindahl index and therefore a more even distribution of higher education R&D.

---

[57] For some countries a part of the data could not be completely broken down into regions. This data is not taken into consideration while computing the Herfindahl index. That is, the shares S_i needed to compute the Herfindahl index are shares in the sum over the regions, instead of shares in the total of the country (the two may differ for some countries).

[58] With the exception of the data for high technology employment, which stem from a study carried out by the Institute for Employment Studies (Jagger and Perryman, 1996).

Table 7.2: The adjusted Herfindahl Index, 1991[59]

	Germany	France	Italy	Greece	Spain	Portugal
High technology employment	0.22	0.18	0.28	NA	0.33	NA
R&D performed by business enterprise	0.30	0.50	0.41	0.56	0.42	0.51
R&D performed by higher education	0.19	0.48	NA	0.21	0.15	0.45
R&D performed by government	NA	0.38	0.51	0.38	0.59	0.90
Total personnel in business enterprise	0.28	0.46	0.38	0.57	0.36	0.52
Total personnel in higher education	0.19	0.27	NA	0.22	0.13	0.43
Total personnel employed by the government	0.22	0.39	0.48	0.35	0.51	0.85
Working population	0.23	0.11	0.07	0.12	0.13	0.34
GDP	0.23	0.17	0.10	0.13	0.13	0.44

Fourth, when taking government R&D into consideration, the results are less clear-cut. The table shows that some countries (like Spain and Italy) are characterized by a very high Herfindahl index with respect to government R&D, that is, government R&D is highly geographically concentrated. In those countries, the Herfindahl index for government R&D is even higher than the Herfindahl index for business enterprise R&D. However, other countries show a Herfindahl index which is below that of business enterprise R&D.

Summarizing the conclusions from Table 7.2, the empirical evidence indicates that high technology employment and R&D performed by business are indeed unevenly distributed over space. The model in Chapters 4 and 6 suggested that the equilibrium pattern in GDP per capita gaps was highly influenced by differences in the learning capability and the exogenous rate of growth of the knowledge stock. The results in this section suggest that these differences do indeed exist across European regions. In terms of the model,

---

[59] NA = Not available. Portugal represents NUTS 3. R&D and GDP are measured in constant prices. A few exceptions had to be made, because of the limited availability of the data. First, the variables HFWP and HFGDPC represent 1989 for Germany. Second, with respect to the R&D data, 1990 is taken for Portugal and 1989 for Germany.

these differences may explain some of the distortions in the pattern of spatial autocorrelation observed in the previous section. Overall, the empirical analysis so far seems to suggest that an explanation of the distribution of GDP per capita over regions based on knowledge spillovers, knowledge generation and learning capability has some plausibility. The empirical results here, however, cannot be considered a full empirical test of the ideas developed in the model of Chapters 4 and 6. For such a test, longer time series than the ones available here are necessary.

3. GEOGRAPHIC SOURCES OF INNOVATIVE ACTIVITY: THE EMPIRICAL RESULTS

Given that differences in business enterprise R&D are important for determining the geographical distribution of GDP per capita gaps, the question arises which factors are related to this variable. This will be the focus of the present section.

One hypothesis, in the (geographical) literature, is that agglomeration in a certain region (that is a region with a high population density) will cause firms to establish R&D intensive businesses in that specific region. A second hypothesis is that the presence of higher education in a region will attract R&D intensive firms (Siebert, 1969) (and thereby increase the ability of the region to absorb and implement new technological knowledge). Using the EUROSTAT region database, several variables which proposedly are correlated to the R&D expenditures of business enterprise are tested for their significance.

One remark needs to be made with respect to causality. The aim of this section is primarily to give evidence for a correlation between business R&D intensity and certain economic phenomena. The direction of the causality of the relationships cannot be demonstrated here, because not enough data was available to make use of time series.

By multiple linear regression, a number of independent variables were combined in order to investigate their relationship to the amount of business R&D expenditure in a region. The dependent variable was measured by two different indicators. The first, IBP89, refers to data on R&D employees in the business sector. It is defined as the share of personnel engaged in R&D performed by business enterprise in the total working population of the region. The second indicator, denoted by IBR89, refers to the R&D intensity of business enterprise, which is measured by the R&D expenditure of business enterprise divided by the gross domestic product (GDP).

With respect to the first hypothesis, the extent to which a region is populated is measured by the working population per area, denoted by WPA89. A second variable which proposedly has an influence on business R&D is denoted by GWPC89, and is defined as gross domestic product in constant prices per head of the working population, (US prices, 1990). GWPC is used as a measure for productivity.

The second goal of the regressions performed in this part of the chapter is to determine to which extent higher education plays a role in inducing business R&D. In order to test for this hypothesis, one variable indicating the amount of higher education in a region is added as a independent variable to the regression equation. The variable denoted by IHP89, is based on total personnel engaged in higher education, while the IHR89 variable is based on R&D expenditure data.

Using these different indicators, two different sets of regressions are presented (see Table 7.3). The first set includes simple linear regressions and has WPA89, GWPC89 and IHP89 (or IHR89) as explaining variables. The second set of regressions adds intercept and slope country dummies to the regression. Each set contains two pairs of regressions, one pair using R&D employment data and the other pair using R&D expenditure data. Each pair contains an equation using only the indicators for population density and increasing returns to scale as explaining variables, and an equation using an additional indicator for higher education.

Based on the correlation matrices for the x-variables of the regressions performed in this section, it can be concluded that multicollinearity might certainly be a problem in assigning values to certain regression parameters. Especially the x-variables with respect to Germany and Greece show large multicollinearity. This result is found in the employee as well as the expenditure data. The observed multicollinearity should be taken into account when analysing the regression results[60].

---

[60] See Appendix B for statistics with respect to multicollinearity.

Table 7.3: Regression results*

	Dependent variable	Independent variables			Constant	R² (Adjusted)	N
		The impact of several variables on R&D expenditures					
1	IBP89	25.39 WPA89 (2.54)	0.26 GWPC89 (4.07)		-5.81 C (-3.35)	0.27 (0.25)	76
2	IBP89	18.01 WPA89 (1.32)	0.45 GWPC89 (1.51)	0.50 IHP89 (5.44)	-11.43 C (-4.87)	0.42 (0.38)	48
3	IBP89	22.62 WPA89 (1.65)	0.48 GWPC89 (5.56)		-10.89 C (-4.58)	0.41 (0.38)	48
4	IBR89	3.34 WPA89 (2.08)	0.06 GWPC89 (5.79)		-0.01 C (-5.18)	0.39 (0.37)	57
5	IBR89	-1.32 WPA89 (-0.52)	0.08 GWPC89 (3.22)	2.68 IHR89 (2.22)	-0.02 C (-3.81)	0.58 (0.53)	28
6	IBR89	1.38 WPA89 (0.49)	0.09 GWPC89 (2.92)		-1.86 C (-3.08)	0.47 (0.43)	28
	Adding DUMMIES						
7	IBP89	-87.34 DEWPA (-2.27)	1.66 DEGWPC (3.68)		-32.66 DDEU (-2.58)	0.80 (0.77)	76
		1.72 FRWPA (0.14)	0.30 FRGWPC (1.31)		-7.24 DFRA (-0.95)		
		11.56 GRWPA (1.27)	0.05 GRGWPC (2.52)		-0.96 DGRE (-2.17)		
		21.44 ESWPA (5.09)	0.14 ESGWPC (2.60)		-3.54 DESP (-2.66)		
		20.17 ITWPA (2.94)	0.17 ITGWPC (3.53)		-5.33 DITA (-4.08)		
8	IBP89	-53.51 DEWPA (-3.47)	1.49 DEGWPC (3.53)	-4.00 DEIHP (-13.37)	-26.58 DDEU (-2.08)	0.87 (0.78)	48
		-20.83 FRWPA (-1.27)	0.30 FRGWPC (1.31)	0.49 FRIHP (1.31)	-5.56 DFRA (-0.73)		
		23.72 GRWPA (4.27)	-0.08 GRGWPC (-2.94)	-0.02 GRIHP (-0.93)	1.19 DGRE (2.40)		
		16.19 ESWPA (3.68)	0.07 ESGWPC (1.36)	0.64 ESIHP (2.27)	-2.64 DESP (-2.58)		

Table 7.3 (continued)

	Dependent variable	Independent variables			Constant	R^2 (Adjusted)	N
9	IBR89	−11.37 DEWPA (−1.88)	0.17 DEGWPC (2.33)		−2.61 DDEU (−1.24)	0.71 (0.61)	57
		−0.54 FRWPA (−0.25)	0.04 FRGWPC (0.94)		−0.42 DFRA (−0.31)		
		2.09 GRWPA (1.89)	0.00 GRGWPC (1.82)		−0.12 DGRE (−1.92)		
		4.14 ESWPA (6.01)	0.02 ESGWPC (2.15)		−0.43 DESP (−2.16)		
10	IBR89	−7.60 DEWPA (−2.31)	0.13 DEGWPC (1.49)	−6.35 DEIHR (−2.75)	0.74 DDEU (0.26)	0.87 (0.56)	28
		4.66 GRWPA (3.24)	−0.02 GRGWPC (−2.31)	0.05 GRIHR (0.58)	0.19 DGRE (1.69)		
		3.86 ESWPA (5.47)	0.01 ESGWPC (1.56)	1.57 ESIHR (1.53)	−0.48 DESP (−2.28)		

Notes: * All regressions are corrected for heteroscedasticity

The first regression indicates a significant WPA and GDPC, which moreover have the expected positive signs. In order to examine the effect of the presence of higher education on the R&D intensity, the IHP89 variable is added to the regression specification. Including higher education results in positive WPA and GDPC coefficients, however, only IHP89 is significant in this relation. However, since there is a serious drop in observations between the two regressions, it is not possible to determine whether the increase in R^2 is due to the drop in datapoints or the adding of the higher education variable. Therefore, in regression 3, the first regression is repeated for the observations available in the second regression. By doing this, the drop in observations is eliminated as a cause for the increase in R^2. The (adjusted) R^2 statistic in regression 3 shows that the IHP89 variable does not change the explanatory power of the regression equation.

The same regressions are repeated for the data on R&D expenditures. This also results in positive and significant values of WPA and GDPC. When higher education is added in the regression specification, this has the expected positive value and is also significantly different from zero[61]. However, the variable for population density loses its significance. Again one regression specification is added to be able to evaluate the effect of an addition of a higher education variable on the R^2. As is shown by regression 6, the most notable impact of the inclusion of the higher education variable in this data set, is the increase in explanatory power of the regression equation.

Introducing slope and intercept country dummies in the second set of regressions leads to another increase in the explanatory power of the regression equations. The regressions in Equations 7 and 8 concern the employee data. Equation 7 shows significant relations for Germany, Spain and Italy. However, the parameters with respect to Germany take an extremely high value; moreover, they have a negative sign. This effect is probably due to the multicollinearity found within this regression specification. When the higher education variable is added in Equation 8, the total number of observations drops from 76 to 48, due to the lack of data for Italy. The regression specification for Germany stays significant, while Spain loses the explanatory power of the intercept dummy for GWPC. This might also be the effect of the observed multicollinearity. It is shown in both regressions that R^2 is quite high. Therefore, it can be concluded that the regression specification fits the data quite well.

---

[61] However, it needs to be said that the regressions presented in the first set were also repeated using logarithms. This worsened the results slightly, but most important variables still stayed significant. Population per area and GDP per capita were also examined as independent variables, instead of using working population and GDP per head of working population. They gave approximately the same results.

Regarding Equations 9 and 10, the use of R&D expenditure data generates similar results. However, using this data set reduces the number of observations severely, because of the lack of business R&D expenditure data for Italy and higher education data for France. When care is taken for the reduction in the degrees of freedom, Equation 9 shows a significant relation for Spain only. The results of Equation 10 suggest that multicollinearity plays a role again. The regression parameters are not significant on the 5 per cent level for any country. However, the R^2 statistic indicates that the regression specification is quite a good fit.

Summarizing the conclusions from Table 7.3, we might say that there is evidence for a positive correlation between population density and business R&D intensity on the one hand; and economic activity and business R&D intensity on the other. The statistical evidence for higher education as an additional explaining variable is also present.

This operation highlights an interesting point, namely that a feedback from GDP per capita to R&D exists. This link was not present in the model in Chapters 4 and 6; however, it might be an interesting suggestion for future research to extent the model in this way.

4. TRANSITION MATRICES

The model in Chapter 4 and 6 analysed the consequences for the pattern of GDP per capita gaps when the differences in learning capability and exogenous rate of growth of the knowledge stock of a region were reduced. This section will focus on the long-run tendencies in business R&D across regions. Here, it will be investigated whether there is any empirical evidence for differences in R&D in the long run. This analysis will be executed using transition matrices (a methodology recently regenerated by Quah (1993) and later repeated by Neven and Gouyette (1995)).

For several EC countries, regional data was available on the personnel engaged in research and development, performed by business enterprise. This is referred to as PB. In addition, data on the working population in each region was available. This variable is denoted by WP[62].

Based upon the number of regions (57), it seemed reasonable to divide the regions into the following three groups. One group contains regions which have a PB/WP lower than one in absolute value. This group was labelled group one. Group two consists of the regions which have a PB/WP between one and three in absolute value. Finally, group three consists of those regions

---

[62] Working population in units of 1000 persons.

which have a PB/WP of more than three. This classification provides for an equal distribution of regions across groups. Hence, the initial distribution of regions is characterized by being approximately one third for each group.

Table 7.4 describes two Markov chain transition matrices, in which the row *j*, column *i* element is the probability that a region in state *i* transits to state *j*.

Table 7.4: Markov chain transition matrices

One year average transition matrix for 1986~1991, 57 regions			
	Group 1	Group 2	Group 3
Group 1 (22)	0.96	0.04	0
Group 2 (15)	0.03	0.93	0.04
Group 3 (20)	0	0.02	0.98
Initial distribution	0.39	0.26	0.35
Ergodic distribution	0.17	0.25	0.58
Five year transition (1986~1991), 57 regions			
Group 1 (22)	0.91	0.09	0
Group 2 (15)	0	0.93	0.07
Group 3 (20)	0	0	1
Initial distribution	0.39	0.26	0.35
Ergodic distribution	0	0	1

The first part of Table 7.4 presents the one year average transition matrix for 1986~1991. This consists of the average of the transition matrices for each one-year-period between 1986 and 1991. The values between brackets give the total number of regions with starting points in that specific group. For example, the element between brackets in the second row of the first panel shows that over the first year (1986) across 57 regions, group 2 consisted of 15 regions, that is, 15 regions had a PB/WP between one and three in absolute value. Of these 15 regions, 2.58 per cent ended up in group 1 at the end of the period (1991), that is, in the group of which the PB/WP rate had declined. Only 4.19 per cent ended up in group 3, and thus had an PB/WP of more than three in absolute value. Thus, out of group 2 a larger percentage caught up (with the regions of group 3), than fell behind (to group 1).

In the one-year average transition matrix, it can easily be seen that all diagonal elements are very close to one and for the first state off the main diagonal all elements are unequal to zero. This result indicates that there is a low transition speed. A simulation showed that the final distribution is only reached after hundreds of years.

Figure 7.4: The distribution across groups over time

Number of regions in group 1, 2 and 3

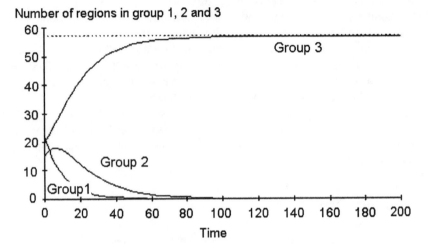

From the ergodic distribution, which is given in the last row of the first panel of Table 7.4, two points emerge. First, compared to the initial distribution (a method indicated by Neven and Gouyette, 1995) it becomes clear that many of the regions in the low R&D group (group 1) have moved to a higher R&D group. In the initial distribution this group (group 1) was still the largest of the three. In the long run this group will become the smallest one. In addition, group 2 becomes smaller in the long run. The third group, which has the largest absolute value of PB/WP, gains members. In the ergodic distribution this group becomes the largest.

Second, complete convergence would be indicated by a distribution in which only one group prevailed (a method suggested by Quah (1993)). This is not the case in the one-year average transition matrix. The results indicate that in the end three groups of different sizes prevail. In the long run there is a tendency for most regions to end up in group 3.

In the five-year transition matrix (see the second panel of Table 7.4) the distribution over the groups in 1986 is compared with the distribution in 1990. This panel also shows diagonal elements which are equal to one, or almost equal to one. So again this is an indication of slow diffusion. It can also clearly be seen from the matrix that in the final distribution only the third group persists. The reason for this is that approximately 6.67 per cent of the regions in group 2 will transit to group 3. However, once in the third group, a region will stay in the third group (the non-diagonal elements in the last row of the matrix are equal to zero). This result would be an indication of convergence. However, since the speed of transition is very low the three groups mentioned above will remain present for a considerable period (see Figure 7.4).

In this respect, it is important to mention that the ergodic distribution of a transition matrix only provides a characterization of the tendencies as embodied in the present configuration of the regions. The final distribution is not a forecast of what will happen, because all kind of disturbances over time ~ like changing government policies or unforeseen events (see Quah, 1993) ~ may cause deviations in the dynamics and therefore in the final distribution.

The results in this section lead to the conclusion that differences in R&D, which was used as an indicator of learning capability and exogenous rate of growth of the knowledge stock, not only exist across European regions, but also tend to persist over time.

5. CONCLUDING REMARKS

This chapter indicated that differences in GDP per capita are present within Europe, which confirms the outcomes of the model developed in Chapters 4 and 6. The south of Germany and the north of Italy form the areas in which the highest GDP per capita of Europe is measured. Moreover, the spatial autocorrelation present in the equilibrium pattern of gaps in the model is also present in the GDP per capita across European regions.

Chapters 4 and 6 pointed out that differences in the learning capability and the exogenous rate of growth of the knowledge stock are important in determining the GDP per capita gaps. More specifically, if such differences exist, they may counteract the tendency for spatial autocorrelation. This chapter explored the geographical distribution of R&D data as an indicator for these parameters. R&D proved to be geographically concentrated to a larger degree than GDP or working population. This indicates that important differences in R&D intensities between regions do indeed exist.

What are the factors that play a role in determining these differences in relation to the learning capability and the exogenous rate of growth of the knowledge stock in a region? Are there certain characteristics of a region that induce a high learning capability? It was found empirically that population density and economic activity are positively correlated to business R&D intensity. In addition, some evidence was found for the presence of higher education in a region as an additional explaining variable. These findings suggest a feedback from GDP to R&D which might be an interesting feature to introduce in the model of this book. This subject will be left for future research.

Finally, attention was directed towards the question whether differences in R&D intensity persist in the long run. The results of this analysis suggested that, based on the present distribution of R&D, differences would continue to exist, at least in the not too long run.

APPENDIX A: NUTS CLASSIFICATION USED IN THIS CHAPTER

G = Regions used in the figures of the GDP per capita in Europe
H = Regions used in the calculation of the Herfindahl Index
R = Regions used in the calculation of the regressions
T = Regions used in the calculation of the transition matrices

NUTS	Country	Region	G	H	R	T
BE2	Belgium	Vlaams Gewest		H		
BE3	Belgium	Region Wallone		H		
BE1	Belgium	Brussel-Bruxelles		H		
DE1	Germany	Baden-Württemberg		H	R	
DE11	Germany	Stuttgart	G			
DE12	Germany	Karlsruhe	G			
DE13	Germany	Freiburg	G			
DE14	Germany	Tübingen	G			
DE2	Germany	Bayern		H	R	
DE21	Germany	Oberbayern	G			
DE22	Germany	Niederbayern	G			
DE23	Germany	Oberpfalz	G			
DE24	Germany	Oberfranken	G			
DE25	Germany	Mittelfranken	G			
DE26	Germany	Unterfranken	G			
DE27	Germany	Schwaben	G			
DE3	Germany	Berlin	G	H	R	
DE4	Germany	Brandenburg	G			
DE5	Germany	Bremen	G	H	R	
DE6	Germany	Hamburg	G	H	R	
DE7	Germany	Hessen		H	R	
DE71	Germany	Darmstadt	G			
DE72	Germany	Giessen	G			
DE73	Germany	Kassel	G			
DE8	Germany	Mecklenburg-Vorpommern	G			
DE9	Germany	Niedersachsen		H	R	

NUTS	Country	Region	G	H	R	T
DE91	Germany	Braunschweig	G			
DE92	Germany	Hannover	G			
DE93	Germany	Lüneburg	G			
DE94	Germany	Weser-Ems	G			
DEA	Germany	Nordrhein-Westfalen		H	R	
DEA1	Germany	Düsseldorf	G			
DEA2	Germany	Köln	G			
DEA3	Germany	Münster	G			
DEA4	Germany	Detmold	G			
DEA5	Germany	Arnsberg	G			
DEB	Germany	Rheinland-Pfalz		H	R	
DEB1	Germany	Koblenz	G			
DEB2	Germany	Trier	G			
DEB3	Germany	Rheinhessen-Pfalz	G			
DEC	Germany	Saarland	G	H	R	
DED	Germany	Sachsen	G			
DEE	Germany	Sachsen-Anhalt				
DEE1	Germany	Dessau	G			
DEE2	Germany	Halle	G			
DEE3	Germany	Magdeburg	G			
DEF	Germany	Schleswig-Holstein	G	H	R	
DEG	Germany	Thüringen	G			
ES1	Spain	Noroeste		H		
ES11	Spain	Galicia	G		R	T
ES12	Spain	Principado de Asturias	G		R	T
ES13	Spain	Cantabria			R	T
ES2	Spain	Noreste		H		
ES21	Spain	Pais Vasco	G		R	T
ES22	Spain	Comunidad Foral de Navarra	G		R	T
ES23	Spain	La Rioja	G		R	T
ES24	Spain	Aragón	G		R	T
ES3	Spain	Comunidad de Madrid	G	H	R	T

NUTS	Country	Region	G	H	R	T
ES4	Spain	Centro (E)		H		
ES41	Spain	Castilla y León	G		R	T
ES42	Spain	Castilla-la Mancha	G		R	T
ES43	Spain	Extremadura	G		R	T
ES5	Spain	Este		H		
ES51	Spain	Cataluña	G		R	T
ES52	Spain	Comunidad Valanciana	G		R	T
ES53	Spain	Islas Baleares			R	T
ES6	Spain	Sur		H		
ES61	Spain	Andalucia	G		R	T
ES62	Spain	Región de Murcia	G		R	T
ES7	Spain	Canarias	G	H	R	T
FR1	France	Ile de France	G	H	R	T
FR2	France	Bassin Parisien		H		
FR21	France	Champagne	G		R	T
FR22	France	Picardie	G		R	T
FR23	France	Haute Normandie	G		R	T
FR24	France	Centre	G		R	T
FR25	France	Basse Normandie	G		R	T
FR26	France	Bourgogne	G		R	T
FR3	France	Nord-Pas-de-Calais	G	H	R	T
FR4	France	Est		H		
FR41	France	Lorraine	G		R	T
FR42	France	Alsace	G		R	T
FR43	France	Franche-Comté	G		R	T
FR5	France	Ouest		H		
FR51	France	Pays de la Loire	G		R	T
FR52	France	Bretagne	G		R	T
FR53	France	Poitou-Charentes	G		R	T
FR6	France	Sud-Ouest		H		
FR61	France	Aquitaine	G		R	T
FR62	France	Midi-Pyrénées	G		R	T
FR63	France	Limousin	G		R	T

NUTS	Country	Region	G	H	R	T
FR7	France	Centre-Est		H		
FR71	France	Rhône-Alpes	G		R	T
FR72	France	Auvergne	G		R	T
FR8	France	Méditerranée		H		
FR81	France	Languedoc-Roussillon	G		R	T
FR82	France	Provence-Alpes-Côte d'Azur	G		R	T
FR9	France	Départements d'outre-mer		H		
IT1	Italy	Nord Ovest		H		
IT11	Italy	Piemonte	G		R	T
IT12	Italy	Valle d'Aosta	G		R	T
IT13	Italy	Liguria	G		R	T
IT2	Italy	Lombardia	G	H	R	T
IT3	Italy	Nord Est		H		
IT31	Italy	Trentino-Alto Adige	G		R	T
IT32	Italy	Veneto	G		R	T
IT33	Italy	Friuli-Venez. Giulia	G		R	T
IT4	Italy	Emilia-Romagna	G	H	R	T
IT5	Italy	Centro (I)		H		
IT51	Italy	Toscana	G		R	T
IT52	Italy	Umbria	G		R	T
IT53	Italy	Marche	G		R	T
IT6	Italy	Lazio	G	H	R	T
IT7	Italy	Abruzzi-Molise		H		
IT71	Italy	Abruzzo	G		R	T
IT72	Italy	Molisse	G			
IT8	Italy	Campania	G	H	R	T
IT9	Italy	Sud		H		
IT91	Italy	Puglia	G		R	T
IT92	Italy	Basilicata	G		R	T
IT93	Italy	Calabria	G		R	T
ITA	Italy	Sicilia	G	H	R	T
ITB	Italy	Sardegna	G	H	R	T

NUTS	Country	Region	G	H	R	T
GR1	Greece	Voreia Ellada		H		
GR11	Greece	Anatoliki Makedonia, Thraki			R	
GR12	Greece	Kentriki Makedonia			R	
GR13	Greece	Dytiki Makedonia			R	
GR14	Greece	Thessalia			R	
GR2	Greece	Kentriki Ellada		H		
GR21	Greece	Ipeiros			R	
GE22	Greece	Ionia Nisia			R	
GR23	Greece	Dytiki Ellada			R	
GR24	Greece	Sterea Ellada			R	
GR25	Greece	Peloponnisos			R	
GR3	Greece	Attiki		H		
GR4	Greece	Nisia Aigaiou, Kriti		H		
GR41	Greece	Voreio Aigaio			R	
GR42	Greece	Notio Aigaio			R	
GR43	Greece	Kriti			R	
PT11	Portugal	Norte	G	H		
PT12	Portugal	Centro (PT)	G	H		
PT13	Portugal	Lisboa e Valo do Tejo	G	H		
PT14	Portugal	Alentejo	G	H		
PT15	Portugal	Algarve	G	H		
PT2	Portugal	Açores		H		
PT3	Portugal	Madeira		H		
NL1	The Netherlands	Noord-Nederland	G			
NL2	The Netherlands	Oost-Nederland	G			
NL3	The Netherlands	West-Nederland	G			
NL4	The Netherlands	Zuid-Nederland	G			
UK1	United Kingdom	North	G			
UK2	United Kingdom	Yorkshire and Humberside	G			
UK3	United Kingdom	East Midlands	G			

NUTS	Country	Region	G	H	R	T
UK4	United Kingdom	East Anglia	G			
UK5	United Kingdom	South East	G			
UK6	United Kingdom	South West	G			
UK7	United Kingdom	West Midlands	G			
UK8	United Kingdom	North West	G			
UK9	United Kingdom	Wales	G			
UKA	United Kingdom	Scotland	G			
UKB	United Kingdom	Northern Ireland	G			
AT11	Austria	Burgenland	G			
AT12	Austria	Niederösterreich	G			
AT13	Austria	Wien	G			
AT21	Austria	Kärnten	G			
AT22	Austria	Steiermark	G			
AT31	Austria	Oberösterreich	G			
AT32	Austria	Salzburg	G			
AT33	Austria	Tirol	G			
AT34	Austria	Vorarlberg	G			

APPENDIX B: MULTICOLLINEARITY

Multicollinearity refers to the feature that occurs when two explaining variables are interacting, and therefore correlated. In that case, the exact influence of one explaining variable on the dependent variable cannot be determined. Were there to be multicollinearity in the regressions performed here, this would make the estimation of the regression parameters less reliable. Usually multicollinearity is accompanied by large standard errors of the parameters, and parameters with wrong signs and values, which obviously makes their explanatory value useless. However, the characteristics of the relationship between dependent and explaining variables are maintained, that is, a high value of the R^2 statistic indicates that the regression specification is a good fit, although the individual regression parameters might be wrong in sign and value.

The following tables represent the correlation matrices for the x-variables of the regressions performed in this section. Two matrices are shown here.

The first, Table 7.5, refers to the regressors of IBP89. The second correlation matrix, Table 7.6, concerns the IBR89-regressors. The terms followed by a country name between brackets indicate the correlation of the slope dummies of the respective variables of that country.

Based on these matrices it can be concluded that multicollinearity might certainly be a problem in assigning values to certain regression parameters. The x-variables with respect to Germany and Greece show large multicollinearity in particular. This result is found in the employee as well as the expenditure data. The observed multicollinearity should be taken into account when analysing the regression results.

Table 7.5: Correlation matrix for the regressors of IBP89

48 observations	*WPA89*	*GWPC89*	*IHP89*
WPA89	1.0000		
GWPC89	0.40558 0.92930 (DE) 0.75544 (FR) 0.96171 (GR) 0.73023 (ES)	1.0000	
IHP89	0.37633 0.93691 (DE) 0.70026 (FR) 0.86750 (GR) 0.83891 (ES)	0.32212 0.97570 (DE) 0.84665 (FR) 0.92092 (GR) 0.89865 (ES)	1.0000

Table 7.6: Correlation matrix for the regressors of IBR89

28 observations	*WPA89*	*GWPC89*	*IHR89*
WPA89	1.0000		
GWPC89	0.73696 0.91942 (DE) 0.95859 (GR) 0.67970 (ES)	1.0000	
IHR89	0.54061 0.90339 (DE) 0.85605 (GR) 0.67136 (ES)	0.45176 0.97032 (DE) 0.91629 (GR) 0.88159 (ES)	1.0000

APPENDIX C: MATHEMATICAL OPERATIONS WITH RESPECT TO THE HERFINDAHL INDEX

The Herfindahl index, by its definition of $\Sigma^{n}_{i=1} S_i^2$, (where S_i denotes the share of the variable of region i in the total of the variable of the country and n is the number of regions in a country) has a minimum value of $1/n$ and a maximum of 1. However, because every country consists of a different amount of regions, the minimum value of the Herfindahl index differs for each country. To be able still to compare the countries, the Herfindahl index is divided by the minimum value it would have in the country under consideration ($1/n$). After this operation, the natural logarithm is taken to give the index a gradual increase (decline) when the degree of concentration gradually becomes higher (lower). However, this new index has a maximum value, which is dependent on the number of regions within a country, namely ln n. Therefore we divide by this value. The result is an index that has a value between 0 and 1.

APPENDIX D: THE GEOGRAPHIC LOCATION OF THE NUTS REGIONS AS USED IN FIGURE 7.1

8. The Geographic Distribution of Patents and Value Added across European Regions

The previous chapter explored regional data on GDP and R&D to give insight into the geographical distribution of GDP per capita gaps and its determinants. The focus was on exploring the extent to which the patterns generated by the model presented earlier in this book resemble those empirically observed. This chapter will take more distance from the model in that it will try to give a more detailed view on the present situation within Europe without focusing too much on the expectations based on the model. In this respect this chapter will direct attention to sector differences (which were assumed to be absent in the model), by exploring data on manufacturing value added and patents.

Section 1 will present the data and the methodology used. Subsequently, in Section 2, an overview will be given of the spatial distribution of innovative activity and production as found in the data. The analysis is similar in Section 3 only now more attention is paid to the geographic location of the innovative regions. Furthermore, differences between sectors are explored. Section 3 contains spatial analysis, paying attention to spillover effects on neighbouring regions. The last section of this chapter will give a brief summary of the results as well as some concluding remarks.

1. DATA AND METHODOLOGY

This chapter tries to identify differences in geographic concentration in innovative activity (proxied by patent applications) and economic activity (proxied by manufacturing value added[63]) over several industries by means of regional data for Europe[64]. Using patents as a proxy for innovative activity

---

[63] Note that there might be important differences between the regional distribution of manufacturing and the regional distribution of services. See for a review on the Central and Capital Cities Region, as identified by the European Commission, van der Knaap and Sleegers (1995).

[64] Appendix B shows the regions that are used in the analysis of this chapter.

has several known disadvantages, which will not all be discussed here. For a good survey of the problems and advantages of the use of patent statistics, see, for example, Pavitt (1985), Basberg (1987) and Griliches (1990).

One problem concerning the use of patents in comparing industrial sectors is that the 'propensity to patent' varies across industries and across countries. The propensity to patent is proxied by dividing the amount of patents per unit by the amount of R&D expenditures in this unit. A unit can represent an industry, but also a country or a region. The lack of disaggregated data on R&D expenditures keeps us from envisaging differences between industries at the regional level. It is commonly known, however, that traditional industries such as industrial electrical equipment, household appliances and stone, clay and glass products, display a relative high propensity to patent (Scherer, 1983, Feldman and Florida, 1994). Industries such as aerospace and other transport (which includes automobile) are characterized by low propensities to patent. These industries devote much of their R&D effort to the building and testing of prototypes and design and these activities do not lead to many patentable inventions (Scherer, 1983). Also the computer industry (office equipment) is characterized by a low propensity to patent. This is mainly because establishing lead times is a more efficient way of protecting innovation in this industry. In general, differences in propensity to patent across sectors are caused by the fact that different sectors make different use of possibilities to protect an innovation.

Table 8.1 gives an indication of the differences in the incidence to patent among the countries under consideration.

Table 8.1: Propensity to patent for 5 European countries

Country	Propensity to patent
Spain	0.39
France	1.55
Italy	1.52
The Netherlands	2.95
United Kingdom	1.33

Source: EPO, EUROSTAT

It is clear from this table that the Netherlands has a very high rate of patents to R&D expenditures, while Spain has an extremely low incidence of patenting. The differences in the propensity to patent across countries ~ as proxied by patents divided by R&D expenditures ~ can stem from several causes. Countries may be specialized in different industries. Some may be specialized in sectors with a traditional high propensity to patent, while others may be focused on sectors with a low propensity to patent. Furthermore, a country with a low propensity to patent can be inefficient in generating innovations from R&D. Another reason might be that R&D is merely used for imitation instead of innovation in such countries. This implies that the analysis in this chapter, unlike the R&D indicator in the previous chapter, is aimed at invention and innovation and not imitation capability.

The data on patents used in this chapter stem from the European Patent Office and are based on the geographic location of the inventor of the patent. The use of patents allocated by the postal code of the inventor make it possible to trace innovative activity back to the region of origin. Another way to approach patent statistics is to use patents according to the location of the applicant. However, this approach is likely to be less reliable in the case of large companies, since patents are filed by the headquarters of a company, even though they might be developed in geographically distant subsidiaries. The object of this study is to get a grasp of the actual location of origin of knowledge in a certain field, making the use of inventors preferable over applicants.

As a proxy for production, manufacturing value added at factor costs is taken. This gives a more accurate image of economic activity than value added at market prices since, in the latter, subsidies and taxes are included, which might differ across countries.

The remainder of this chapter is devoted to spatial patterns of economic and innovative activity as they can be found in the EUROSTAT REGIO database. In doing so these data are combined with patent statistics developed on the basis of data of the European Patent Office (EPO). EPO classifies patents by field of technology according to the International Patent Classification (IPC). To compare patent data to economic data the technology fields were assigned to economic sectors as classified by the International Standard Industrial Classification of All Economic Activities (ISIC – rev. 2) of the United Nations. This concordance was taken from Verspagen, van Moergastel and Slabbers (1994). They have used the main notation of the patent publication. This identifies the invention in its key aspect. Verspagen, van Moergastel and Slabbers (1994) allocated all IPC subclasses (concerning manufacturing) to 22 ISIC sectors (manufacturing). In several cases a subclass is allocated partly to one ISIC sector and partly to one or more other ISIC sectors. The concordance between ISIC and NACE-CLIO (the latter is the classification used by EUROSTAT) is given in Appendix C.

2. SPATIAL DISTRIBUTION OF PATENTS AND VALUE ADDED ACROSS EUROPEAN REGIONS

In the previous chapter, it was shown that business R&D was unevenly distributed across space. No attention was paid to the location of the innovative regions, however. This section will show the geographic location of the innovative regions within Europe. In this section the location of innovative regions will be compared to the location of the regions with high economic activity. The geographic distribution of patents and manufacturing value added in Europe over the years 1986~1990 is displayed in Figures 8.1 and 8.2.

It should be kept in mind that the sample used in this chapter does not include German regions, even though recent studies (Paci and Usai, 1998; Verspagen, 1997; Breschi, 1995) have found that the most innovative regions of Europe are located in Germany. The primary reason for not including Germany was that no data on value added were available for this country. Also, the inclusion of German patent data could possibly distort an objective view. The fact that the EPO is located in Germany means as a consequence, that German firms can be over-represented. EPO regulations closely follow the granting procedures of the German national system and therefore it is relatively easy for a German firm to apply to EPO (Paci and Usai, 1998).

As Figure 8.1 points out, the geographic distribution of patenting activity is highly concentrated across regions. High patenting activity is located in the north of Italy, with a branch to Rhône-Alpes and Paris, the south and west of The Netherlands and the south of the United Kingdom. Each of these regions performs at least two per cent of European patenting. The top twelve regions account for about 70 per cent of the total number of patents (Table 8.2), which indicates a high geographic concentration in only a few European regions. It is notable that Spain and the southern part of Italy display very little patent activity. Figure 8.2 shows that manufacturing value added is similarly concentrated across European regions; however, at first sight less than patents.

Figure 8.1: Share in European patenting

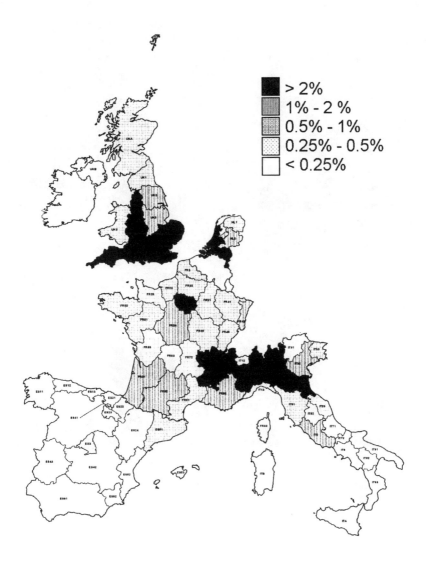

Legend:
- > 2%
- 1% - 2 %
- 0.5% - 1%
- 0.25% - 0.5%
- < 0.25%

Source: EPO

Figure 8.2: Share in European manufacturing value added

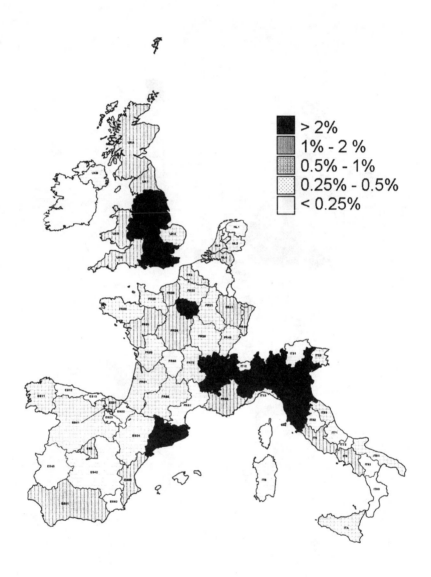

Source: EUROSTAT

Figure 8.3: Patents corrected for population

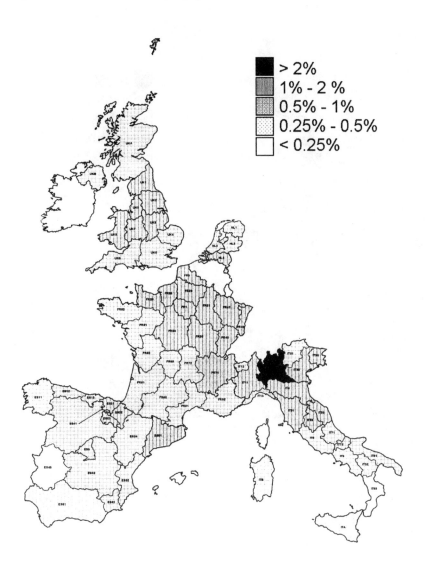

Source: EPO, EUROSTAT

Figure 8.4: Value added corrected for population

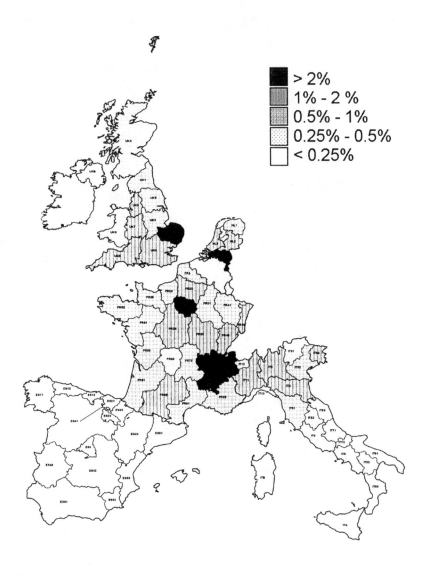

Source: EUROSTAT

Table 8.2, which shows that about half of European value added is generated by the top twelve regions, confirms this observation. Comparing the spatial location of concentration of patents and manufacturing value added (Table 8.2), only a few differences can be observed. Almost all regions appear on both listings, although they might differ in ranking. The regions that disappear from one of the listings turn up at the 14th or 17th rank if the complete listing is considered. This finding indicates that the most innovative regions are the same regions in which most of the European value added is generated.

Table 8.2: Distribution of patents and value added by region

Region	Share in European patenting	Region	Share in European value added
Ile de France (FR1)	18.0	Lombardia (IT2)	8.3
South East (UK5)	13.0	Ile de France (FR1)	6.5
Lombardia (IT2)	6.8	South East (UK5)	6.5
Rhône-Alpes (FR71)	6.7	Piemonte (IT11)	3.8
Zuid Nederland (NL3)	6.4	Cataluna (ES51)	3.3
West Nederland (NL3)	4.3	Veneto (IT32)	3.3
North West (UK8)	2.9	North West (UK8)	3.2
Piemonte (IT11)	2.7	Rhône-Alpes (FR71)	3.1
West Midlands (UK7)	2.4	Emilia-Romagna (IT4)	3.0
South West (UK6)	2.3	West Midlands (UK7)	3.0
East Anglia (UK4)	2.2	West Nederland (NL3)	2.4
Emilia-Romagna (IT4)	2.0	Yorkshire and Humberside (UK2)	2.4
Total	69.7	Total	48.8

Source: EPO, EUROSTAT

However, the simple comparison of the amount of patents across regions is not entirely correct, because it ignores the fact that the size of the population (the manufacturing base) of some regions is larger than in other regions (Audretsch and Feldman, 1996). Therefore, in Figure 8.3 the amount of patents of a region divided by the average population[65] of the region over the 5 years under consideration (1986~1990) is compared to the European total amount of patents divided by the average of European population. Figure 8.4 does the same for manufacturing value added. The darkest areas in the Figures 8.3 and 8.4 show regions which have a number of patents (value

---

[65] It would have been preferable to correct patents for manufacturing employment. However, since the correlation between population and manufacturing employment is very high (the correlation does not differ significantly from 1 at the 5 per cent significance level) this would probably not have made much difference.

added) per head which is at least twice as high as the overall European ratio. The dark grey areas still have more than average patents (value added) per head. It can clearly be seen that the patent data show more regions with extreme values (black and white areas) than the data for value added, which display a more dispersed pattern in the sense that almost all regions are grey. These findings indicate that value added is less concentrated than patenting[66]. This is not a great surprise, since it is commonly known that research institutes (private as well as public) and R&D departments of large enterprises are not as widely spread as production.

The conclusion that can be drawn from the data is that both patents and value added show some degree of concentration over Europe, although patents more than value added. However, when Figure 8.1 and Figure 8.2 are compared it can also be concluded that the location of the patent- and manufacturing value added-intensive regions does not differ greatly. The empirically observed patterns seem to confirm the findings of Chapter 7 that differences in economic activity as well as innovative activity exist across European regions. This corresponds to the expectations derived from the model developed in Chapters 4 and 6.

Although Figures 8.1 and 8.2 display the geographic distribution of innovative as well as economic activity in Europe, they aggregate across all industries and therefore overlook sectoral differences. The question arises whether differences exist when looking at a sectoral level.

The Herfindahl index is used to indicate whether a variable is distributed evenly or concentrated geographically. Here, the specification used in Chapter 7 is made sector specific:

$$HF_j = 1 + \frac{\ln \sum_{i=1}^{n} S_{ij}^2}{\ln n},$$

(8.1)

where HF_j denotes the rescaled Herfindahl index for sector j, S_{ij} denotes the share of a variable of region i and sector j in the total of the variable of a country in sector j. A value of one in the resulting index represents evidence of complete geographical concentration in one region, while a value of zero represents evidence of equal distribution of the variable under consideration.

When the Herfindahl is calculated for each industry in Europe, the results differ for the geographic distribution of value added in comparison with the geographic distribution of patents (Figure 8.5). It is again shown that patents display a higher degree of concentration than value added. However, value added shows more variety in concentration across sectors, while for patents

---

[66] The evidence of Paci and Usai (1998) confirms this finding.

all the sectors are concentrated to approximately the same extent. With regard to value added, the sectors B42 (textiles and clothing, leather and footwear)[67] and B47 (wood, paper and printing) display a more than average geographic concentration. The geographic concentration of the population within Europe is also displayed in Figure 8.5. Comparing patent activity and value added to the concentration of the population (which is assumed to be evenly distributed across regions) one can observe that both variables display a higher concentration.

Figure 8.5: Herfindahl index for Europe per sector

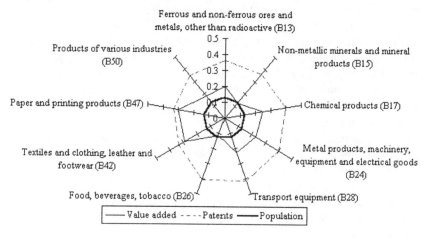

Source: EPO, EUROSTAT

When we take a look at what the Herfindahl index tells us for the individual countries, we observe that within a country geographic concentrations of industries are more profound than within Europe as a whole, suggesting that at the country level more intensive clustering of activity takes place. Figure 8.6 displays the Herfindahl index for each sector within each available country. The horizontal line shows the Herfindahl index for population in each country. Notable is the large patenting concentration of the Spanish B42 sector (textiles). The other Spanish industries are also very concentrated with regard to innovative activity. Within the Netherlands, large differences between industries are visible. While B13 (ferrous and non-ferrous ores and metals, other than radioactive) is highly concentrated with regard to patents as well as value added, B15 (minerals) is as dispersed as

---

[67] For a description of the NACE CLIO sector codes, see Appendix A.

population. Overall, these results confirm the earlier results that within Europe value added is more dispersed than patents, while in most cases both variables are more concentrated than population.

When Figure 8.6 is compared to Figure 8.5, it can clearly be seen that, within countries, sectors are much more concentrated than in Europe as a whole. For patents, and to a lesser extent also for value added, the European Herfindahl index is low compared to the country specific indexes.

Concluding, within Europe evidence is found of geographic concentration of economic activity and technology. Within countries geographic concentration is more profound. We would expect that in a united Europe, one could already observe the concentration of industries in different parts of Europe. One would expect firms to have already chosen the best location among all European regions. Apparently, they do so only to a limited extent. This may be attributed to the impact of national systems of innovation (NSI). In each country, organizations such as firms and research institutes interact in a different manner with each other and with the government sector in producing and distributing knowledge. The existence of different national systems of innovation has as a consequence that knowledge spills over more easily across regions within a country than across country borders. Therefore, the above observation underpins the analysis in Chapter 6 (Section 3.2: Barriers to knowledge spillovers). NSIs have an influence on the distribution of growth across nations and regions. However, it is expected that the process of European integration could affect the NSIs in Europe and might eventually lead to the emergence of a European system of innovation (Johnson and Gregersen, 1997).

In order to pinpoint the location of country specific concentrations, Table 8.3 shows the sectors that are most important within each country with respect to patenting and to value added. Of each sector the three regions with the largest share in a country's total are displayed. It can be observed that sector concentrations differ among regions.

For instance, observe the shaded area in the table. It shows the metal products sector (B24) in France. This sector accounts for the majority (64.4 per cent) of total patenting in France. Moreover, the table indicates that in each country metal products is the sector with the highest activity with respect to patents (as well as value added). Ile de France (FR1) holds most of all French patents in this sector (47.6 per cent). In fact, the three most patent-intensive French regions within this sector hold 67.7 per cent of total patents. This indicates that the metal products sector is largely concentrated within a few regions in France.

Figure 8.6: Herfindahl index for each country per sector

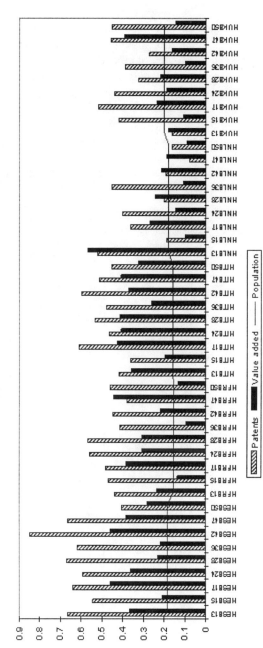

Source: EPO, EUROSTAT

161

The table allows us to compare the results for patents to those for manufacturing value added. In France, the metal products sector represents only 31 per cent of the total of the country value added. This again points to the feature that patenting is much more concentrated than value added. Note that Ile de France generates only 28.2 per cent of French value added in this sector. The other countries show similar distributions.

From this table it can be concluded that innovative activities are highly concentrated in a single region within each country. The same, although to a lesser extent, holds for manufacturing value added.

Table 8.3: Most important sectors and regions within a country (corrected for population)

Country	Most important sector according to patents	Share in total country industry	Most important regions	Share in industry	Most important sector according to value added	Share in total country industry	Most important regions	Share in industry
Spain	B24	56.3	ES51	49.9	B24	21.7	ES51	28.7
			ES3	25.6			ES21	19.8
			ES21	6.1			ES3	18.7
	B17	19.2	ES51	52.9	B36	19.5	ES51	20.8
			ES3	28.4			ES61	18.2
			ES61	5.9			ES3	9.7
	B28	11	ES51	60	B42	10.3	ES51	38.1
			ES3	17.2			ES52	24.8
			ES21	8.5			ES3	8.4
France	B24	64.4	FR1	47.6	B24	31	FR1	28.2
			FR71	15.7			FR71	14.7
			FR82	4.4			FR51	5.1
	B17	15.5	FR1	37.8	B36	13.8	FR1	13
			FR71	22.5			FR52	9.1
			FR42	5.6			FR71	8
	B28	9.5	FR1	49.7	B28	12.2	FR1	29.9
			FR71	8.2			FR43	7.7
			FR43	5.2			FR71	6.3
Italy	B24	59.1	IT2	38	B24	28.8	IT2	33.9
			IT11	14.1			IT11	13.5

Table 8.3 continued

			IT4	13.3			IT4	13.5
	B17	19.1	IT2	52.7	B42	16.4	IT2	28.2
			IT11	10.8			IT32	15.9
			IT4	9.2			IT51	15.3
	B28	9.8	IT11	36.8	B50	10.7	IT2	26.7
			IT2	31.1			IT32	16
			IT4	8.2			IT11	10.8
Netherlands	B24	67.8	NL4	60.2	B24	28.1	NL4	38.8
			NL3	23.7			NL3	33
			NL2	12.2			NL2	20.1
	B17	16.7	NL3	56.2	B17	20.1	NL3	50.4
			NL4	28.2			NL4	29.2
			NL2	12.9			NL2	14.1
	B36	5.4	NL3	64.1	B36	16.9	NL3	40
			NL4	20.2			NL4	26.4
			NL2	12			NL2	20.9
UK	B24	61.6	UK5	47.3	B24	30.9	UK5	27.9
			UK6	9.4			UK7	15.3
			UK4	8.9			UK8	9.8
	B17	20.1	UK5	52.5	B36	13	UK5	19.6
			UK8	15			UK8	13.4
			UK2	6			UKA	12.1
	B28	7.1	UK5	33.6	B17	10.7	UK5	27.8
			UK7	23.6			UK8	20.9
			UK6	12.5			UK1	11.6

Inspired by Audretsch and Feldman (1994).
Source: EPO, EUROSTAT.

The Revealed Comparative Advantage index (RTA) was calculated in order to give insight into the extent of the specialization of a region in an industry. This index is defined as

$$(P_{ij}/\sum_{j}P_{ij})/(\sum_{i}P_{ij}/\sum_{i}\sum_{j}P_{ij}),$$

where P denotes the number of patents in region i and sector j. To standardize this RTA-index to the interval $[-1,1]$ we calculate $(RTA-1)/(RTA+1)$. For all regions documented in Table 8.3 the RTA reaches a value round and about 0.98 (not documented separately) which indicates considerable regional specialization.

In sum, the analysis conducted so far has given several results. First, regions that are the most innovative in terms of patent activity have the highest share in manufacturing value added as well. Second, production is more dispersed than innovative activity; however, both are geographically concentrated (when compared to the distribution of population) across European regions. With respect to patenting, all sectors are concentrated to approximately the same extent at the European level, while manufacturing value added shows clear differences in sectoral concentration. Third, at the country level clustering of sectors occurs to a higher extent than at the European level. Geographic patterns of innovation as well as production differ across sectors at the country level, suggesting that country-specific factors in combination with sector-specific factors play an important role in determining the geographic pattern of innovation and production across countries.

3. SPATIAL ANALYSIS

In this section, we will address our attention to spatial autocorrelation (Cliff and Ord, 1973, see also Chapter 7) in the data. In Chapter 7, it was demonstrated that, according to the model described in Chapters 4 and 6, differences in knowledge generation and learning capability (proxied by R&D intensity) have an influence on the distribution of economic activity (Section 3). It was found that differences in these parameters exist across regions. In the model developed earlier, these differences were assumed (for simplicity) to be purely random. In reality, however, we may find that differences in innovative activity are systematic. This section will investigate whether spatial autocorrelation is found in patents and value added. Again, we will distinguish between sectors.

In Figure 8.7 the results for the evolution over time of the coefficient of Moran for the total of all sectors is shown. Note that the observations for value added only start in 1985. No appreciable trend can be identified. The importance of spillovers stays the same throughout time. Therefore, for the rest of this paragraph attention will only be paid to the five year period of our sample (1986~1990).

In Table 8.4 the coefficient of Moran for patents and value added (corrected for population) is compared. The table indicates that patents show a respectable degree of spatial autocorrelation in almost all sectors. Looking at value added, significant autocorrelation can only be found in four sectors, indicating that geographic clustering plays a more important role in innovative activity than in the generation of value added.

Figure 8.7: Coefficient of Moran for the total of all sectors

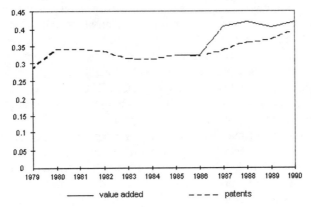

Source: EPO, EUROSTAT

Table 8.4: Moran per NACE sector

Sector	Patents		Value added	
Ferrous and non-ferrous ores and metals, other than radioactive (B13)	0.12	(1.17)	0.05	(0.53)
Non-metallic minerals and mineral products (B15)	0.27*	(2.40)	0.19	(1.79)
Chemical products (B17)	0.27*	(2.46)	0.19	(1.77)
Metal products, machinery, equipment and electrical goods (B24)	0.29*	(2.59)	0.35*	(3.11)
Transport equipment (B28)	0.31*	(2.75)	0.13	(1.25)
Food, beverages, tobacco (B36)	0.38*	(3.36)	0.18	(1.67)
Textiles and clothing, leather and footwear (B42)	0.18	(1.67)	0.23*	(2.07)
Paper and printing products (B47)	0.29*	(2.64)	0.33*	(2.92)
Products of various industries (B50)	0.36*	(3.20)	0.32*	(2.89)
Total (B30)	0.36*	(3.21)	0.42*	(3.69)

Notes: Values between brackets indicate t-values * significant at the 5% level
Source: EPO, EUROSTAT

With respect to patents the data allow us to disaggregate to ISIC classes in order to observe the origin of the significance of the Moran coefficient in the broader NACE classification. Table 8.5 clearly shows the sectors for which a significant coefficient of Moran is found, indicating that these sectors are clustered over region borders. It is notable that sectors which are significant under the NACE classification are composed of ISIC sectors which are not all significant[68]. This leads to the impression that when certain ISIC sectors with a low coefficient of Moran are grouped together in the NACE classification, a higher coefficient of Moran might occur simply because these different ISIC sectors are located in regions close together. Thus, the whole spectrum of chemical ISIC sectors (ZCC, ZCD, ZCP and ZLR) might group together in one location, which causes a high coefficient of Moran for the chemical sector in the NACE classification (B17), while the individual ISIC sectors do not display high clustering over regions, simply because they are located closer to other chemical sectors rather than to their own sector.

It is notable that high-tech sectors like ZHO (office machines and computers), ZCD (pharmaceuticals) and ZEC (communication equipment and semiconductors) display a very low coefficient of Moran (which is not significant), indicating that within Europe there is little clustering of these sectors in a group of regions located close to each other. This impression is reinforced when the coefficient of Moran is determined for a different grouping of ISIC sectors which can be labelled as high-tech, medium-tech and low-tech. Table 8.5 indicates that high-tech sectors display the lowest degree of clustering, in contrast to medium- and low-tech sectors in which spatial clustering is more profound. Probably the clustering in high-tech sectors is very intensive and will therefore not cover a group of regions but stay within one region. The Herfindahl index could give some more information on this issue. From Figure 8.8 it can be seen that all high-tech sectors do indeed display very high concentration across European regions. In fact, all sectors (except shipbuilding, which is spatially dependent on a sea-bounded region and electrical machinery) display a lower geographic concentration than the high-tech sectors, indicating that high-tech is indeed concentrated in only a few regions in Europe.

From the spatial analysis, it can be concluded that economic as well as innovative activity clusters within groups of contiguous regions. At the sectoral level clear differences appear. It has been shown that with respect to innovative activity low-tech sectors display the highest degree of clustering within groups of regions. High-tech sectors on the other hand show low coefficients of Moran. When this result is combined with very high

---

[68] The concordance between NACE and ISIC is given in Appendix C.

Herfindahl indexes for these sectors, it can be concluded that high-tech sectors concentrate geographically in only a few regions in Europe, and these clusters do not extend beyond region borders.

Table 8.5: Coefficient of Moran per ISIC sector

Sector	Moran			Moran	
Instruments (ZHI)	0.29*	(2.60)			
Pharmaceuticals (ZCD)	0.16	(1.50)			
Communication equipment and semiconductors (ZEC)	0.08	(0.82)	High Tech	0.20	(1.87)
Office machines and computers (ZHO)	0.05	(0.51)			
Aerospace (ZAE)	0.01	(0.21)			
Industrial chemicals (ZCC)	0.29*	(2.58)			
Non-electrical machinery (ZHN)	0.39*	(3.49)			
Electrical machinery (ZEM)	0.10	(0.99)	Medium Tech	0.37*	(3.30)
Motor vehicles (ZTM)	0.29*	(2.58)			
Other transport (ZTO)	0.26*	(2.36)			
Stone, clay and glass (ZOG)	0.27*	(2.40)			
Non-ferrous metals (ZMN)	0.18	(1.65)			
Petroleum refineries (ZCP)	0.23*	(2.05)			
Rubber and plastics (ZLR)	0.36*	(3.19)			
Basic metals (ZMD)	0.49*	(4.34)			
Ferrous metals (ZMF)	0.08	(0.82)	Low Tech	0.51*	(4.49)
Shipbuilding (ZTI)	0.15	(1.41)			
Food, drink and tobacco (ZLF)	0.38*	(3.36)			
Textiles, footwear and leather (ZLX)	0.18	(1.67)			
Wood, cork and furniture (ZOW)	0.29*	(2.64)			
Other manufacturing industries (ZOO)	0.35*	(3.12)			
Paper and printing (ZOP)	0.27*	(2.42)			

Notes: values between brackets indicate t-values, * significant at the 5% level
Source: EPO

Figure 8.8: Herfindahl index for Europe

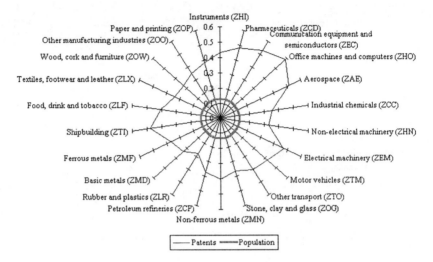

Source: EPO

4. CONCLUSIONS

The main objective of this chapter was to give a detailed sectoral view on the present situation within Europe with respect to the location and the distribution of economic and innovative activity. In doing so, innovative activity is proxied by patenting activity by inventor, whereas manufacturing value added at factor costs is used as a proxy for economic activity. In general, regions that have a large geographic concentration of patents also tend to have a large concentration of value added. However, innovative activity is geographically concentrated to a larger extent than value added. This seems to point to some sort of increasing returns to location.

If a sectoral perspective is taken, one finds clear evidence of geographic concentrations of innovative as well as economic activity in that for most sectors these variables are more concentrated than population. This holds when Europe as a whole is observed. However, when looking at the country level, even more profound geographic concentration within sectors occurs. The extent to which geographic concentration plays a role differs across sectors, indicating that industry-specific as well as country-specific conditions determine the spatial pattern of innovation and production.

The mere analysis of concentrations does not give any indication as to spillover effects of either innovative or economic activity due to the proximity of one or several active regions. By applying the coefficient of Moran to the dataset, the results point in the direction that such spillover effects do take place for both types of activity in several sectors. Especially, innovative activity shows a large degree of spatial autocorrelation in the majority of sectors, mainly low-tech and medium-tech sectors. High-tech sectors, however, are found to be highly concentrated in few regions, which are not contiguous.

The evidence for spillover effects seems to suggest that locally bounded knowledge spillovers and agglomeration economies play an important role. Furthermore, since innovative and economic concentrations are largely located in the same regions, it seems to be the case that both activities reinforce each other.

Since this chapter has been descriptive in nature and no time series were available to give a more profound analysis of the underlying mechanisms, the findings only allow for some speculation on these underlying economic mechanisms. A consequence of the increasing returns to innovative and economic activity seems to be that some regions might lock into a low productivity ~ low innovation situation ~ while others endure high economic and innovative activity. This geographic pattern indicates no convergence across European regions. Cumulative causation together with the presence of spillover effects lie at the root of this pattern. Region-specific policies might strengthen a region's weak position by increasing its learning capability and knowledge generation. On the other hand, these findings suggest that NSIs still have a large influence on the regional patterns in GDP per capita gaps and knowledge. This might be an encouragement to European policymakers to stimulate a European system of innovation.

APPENDIX A: NACE CLASSIFICATION

B13	Ferrous and non-ferrous ores and metals, other than radioactive
B15	Non-metallic minerals and mineral products
B17	Chemical products
B24	Metal products, machinery, equipment and electrical goods
B28	Transport equipment
B36	Food, beverages, tobacco
B42	Textiles and clothing, leather and footwear
B47	Paper and printing products
B50	Products of various industries

APPENDIX B: REGIONS USED IN THE ANALYSIS

No.	*NUTS*	*Country*	*Region*
1	ES11	Spain	Galicia
2	ES12	Spain	Principado de Asturias
3	ES13	Spain	Cantabria
4	ES21	Spain	Pais Vasco
5	ES22	Spain	Comunidad Foral de Navarra
6	ES23	Spain	La Rioja
7	ES24	Spain	Aragón
8	ES3	Spain	Comunidad de Madrid
9	ES41	Spain	Castilla y León
10	ES42	Spain	Castilla-la Mancha
11	ES43	Spain	Extremadura
12	ES51	Spain	Cataluña
13	ES52	Spain	Comunidad Valanciana
14	ES61	Spain	Andalucia
15	ES62	Spain	Región de Murcia
16	ES7	Spain	Canarias
17	FR1	France	Ile de France
18	FR21	France	Champagne
19	FR22	France	Picardie

No.	NUTS	Country	Region
20	FR23	France	Haute Normandie
21	FR24	France	Centre
22	FR25	France	Basse Normandie
23	FR26	France	Bourgogne
24	FR3	France	Nord-Pas-de Calais
25	FR41	France	Lorraine
26	FR42	France	Alsace
27	FR43	France	Franche-Comté
28	FR51	France	Pays de la Loire
29	FR52	France	Bretagne
30	FR53	France	Poitou-Charentes
31	FR61	France	Aquitaine
32	FR62	France	Midi-Pyrénées
33	FR63	France	Limousin
34	FR71	France	Rhône-Alpes
35	FR72	France	Auvergne
36	FR81	France	Languedoc-Roussillon
37	FR82	France	Provence-Alpes-Côte d'Azur
38	IT11	Italy	Piemonte
39	IT12	Italy	Valle d'Aosta
40	IT13	Italy	Liguria
41	IT2	Italy	Lombardia
42	IT31	Italy	Trentino-Alto Adige
43	IT32	Italy	Veneto
44	IT33	Italy	Friuli-Venez. Giulia
45	IT4	Italy	Emilia-Romagna
46	IT51	Italy	Toscana
47	IT52	Italy	Umbria
48	IT53	Italy	Marche
49	IT6	Italy	Lazio
50	IT71	Italy	Abruzzo
51	IT72	Italy	Molisse
52	IT8	Italy	Campania
53	IT91	Italy	Puglia
54	IT92	Italy	Basilicata
55	IT93	Italy	Calabria

No.	NUTS	Country	Region
56	ITa	Italy	Sicilia
57	ITb	Italy	Sardegna
58	NL1	The Netherlands	Noord-Nederland
59	NL2	The Netherlands	Oost-Nederland
60	NL3	The Netherlands	West-Nederland
61	NL4	The Netherlands	Zuid-Nederland
62	UK1	United Kingdom	North
63	UK2	United Kingdom	Yorkshire and Humberside
64	UK3	United Kingdom	East Midlands
65	UK4	United Kingdom	East Anglia
66	UK5	United Kingdom	South East
67	UK6	United Kingdom	South West
68	UK7	United Kingdom	West Midlands
69	UK8	United Kingdom	North West
70	UK9	United Kingdom	Wales
71	UKa	United Kingdom	Scotland
72	UKb	United Kingdom	Northern Ireland

APPENDIX C: CONCORDANCE BETWEEN NACE-CLIO AND ISIC

Table 8.6 gives the concordance between NACE-CLIO (value added data) and ISIC as is used in this chapter. An additional column is added to indicate whether a sector is high, medium or low tech.

Table 8.6: Concordance between NACE-CLIO and ISIC

NACE				ISIC	
B13	Basic metals	ZMF	Basic metals, ferrous	371	Low
		ZMN	Basic metals, non-ferrous	372	Low
B15	Non-metallic mineral products ('Stone, clay and glass')	ZOG	Non-metallic mineral products ('Stone, clay and glass')	36	Low
B17	Chemicals	ZCC	Chemicals and chemical products (less pharmaceuticals)	351+352–3522	Med.
		ZCD	Pharmaceuticals	3522	High

		ZCP	Coke, refined petroleum products and nuclear fuel	353+354	Low
		ZLR	Rubber and plastic products	355+356	Low
B24	Metal and electrics	ZMD	Fabricated metal products (except machinery and equipment)	381	Low
		ZHN	Other machinery	382–3825	Med.
		ZHO	Office, accounting and computing machinery	3825	High
		ZEC	Electronic equipment	3832	High
		ZEM	Electrical machinery	383–3832	Med.
		ZHI	Medical, precision and optical instruments, watches and clocks (instruments)	385	High
B28	Transport	ZTI	Shipbuilding	3841	Low
		ZTM	Automobiles	3843	Med.
		ZTO	Other transport	384–3841– 3843–3845	Med.
		ZAE	Aerospace	3845	High
B36	Food, beverages and tobacco	ZLF	Food, beverages and tobacco	31	Low
B42	Textiles, wearing apparel, fur and leather	ZLX	Textiles, wearing apparel, fur and leather	32	Low
B47	Wood, paper, printing, publishing	ZOW	Wood, paper, printing, publishing	331+34	Low
B50	Manufacturing	ZOO	Other manufacturing	39	Low
		ZOP	Furniture	332	Low

9. A Concluding Summary

The aim of this book has been to implement concepts from geography into a technology gap model and thereby broaden the understanding of knowledge spillovers (across space). More precisely, the impact of local knowledge spillovers on regional growth has been analysed. The book explored three key areas. First, Chapters 2 and 3 examined the literature on diffusion of knowledge and provided a methodological framework. Chapters 4 to 6 focused on analysing the influence of local knowledge spillovers on regional gaps, and were devoted to setting up a model that gives an impression of these effects. The implications of the model were explored by means of simulation techniques. Chapters 7 and 8 dealt with the current situation in Europe, using empirical analyses to demonstrate regional gaps and differences in economic and innovative activity across regions.

This chapter will give a concluding summary of all issues raised by the book. In addition, attention will be given to the policy implications of the results brought forward. The last section will try to outline some proposals for future research.

1. SUMMARY AND CONCLUSIONS

Chapter 2 gave a (selective) survey of the literature on diffusion of knowledge. The chapter reviewed the perspective on knowledge spillovers in various strands in the literature. Whereas traditional neo-classical growth models assume knowledge to be immediately available everywhere, cumulative causation theories adopt the idea that knowledge will stay in the geographical place from which it originates and will not spread at all. 'In between' are imperfect diffusion theories, which assume knowledge to spread gradually over time and space. From these contributions, we obtained elements for a regional model on knowledge spillovers. One element was taken from technology gap theory, which assumes that technological distance plays an essential part in determining the growth rates of countries (the technology gap literature mainly considers countries, although some regional models exist). A second element was taken from the geographical literature on agglomeration effects and growth poles. In this literature, geographical distance plays a very important role in that increasing returns to location are assumed. The geographical agglomeration of industrial activities leads to a set of advantages that induces further agglomeration. Among these advantages are the availability of skilled labour and intermediate goods' suppliers, as well as the easy transmission and discussion of new ideas. In this book, the focus lay on this last factor. Knowledge spillovers are assumed to take place more easily across smaller geographical distances.

In Chapter 3, evolutionary theory was presented as an apt way to model regional knowledge spillovers. The merits of an evolutionary approach lie in the acknowledgement of the heterogeneity of agents. We assumed that reality can be best approximated by a model that takes into account the fact that regions differ in several respects. Regions were assumed to differ in their behaviour with respect to efficiency in implementing knowledge spillovers from other regions and in generating their own knowledge base. These factors, which might be shaped by, for example, historical influences, may have an impact on the distribution of growth across regions. Starting with the notion that regions are initially very different in their behaviour, and following evolutionary theory, we introduced a selection mechanism that determines the growth rate of regions. Chapter 3 introduced the Goodwin model as capturing the main evolutionary ideas.

Chapter 4 developed a simple model for knowledge spillovers across regions. Spatial issues such as increasing returns to location were integrated into a technology gap model. Knowledge spillovers were assumed to be influenced by two different factors. First, it was assumed that proximity and location play an essential role in the transmission of knowledge between regions. Therefore, the geographical distance relative to another region is an important factor that determines the amount of knowledge spillovers. A second factor is technological distance, that is, the technology gap. This term refers to the extent to which a region is able to assimilate knowledge from other regions at each moment in time. Technological distance is measured by the level of the knowledge stock of one region relative to the level of the knowledge stock of another region.

Several parameters have an influence on the equilibrium gap of a region. Two of them were highlighted. First, differences in the exogenous rate of knowledge generation across regions have an influence on the equilibrium gap. An increase in the rate of knowledge generation in a backward region could be established by devoting more efforts to R&D. The result will be that the backward region experiences a lower gap with respect to the leader region. In other words, the backward region catches up. The second factor is the learning capability, which denotes the intrinsic capability of a region to implement knowledge from other regions. This concept differs from technological distance in that the learning capability is a characteristic of a region that is modelled as an exogenous factor. A relatively high learning capability can also lead to catch-up in an otherwise backward region.

The main contribution of the model outlined is that it allows spatial factors to have an influence on catching up and falling behind. The model can be analysed by simulations.

The results from these simulations were reviewed in Chapter 5. Heterogeneity in regions was introduced by allowing regions to differ with respect to an initial stock variable and several parameters. More precisely, experiments were carried out in which regions differed with respect to the initial level of the knowledge stock, the learning capability and the exogenous rate of knowledge generation across regions. The geographical location of a region played a role in every experiment. Several geographical spheres were considered. We consider a lattice of honeycombs, a column and a globe. The first of these spheres is two-dimensional. There is exactly one central region. This region has a favourable location for receiving knowledge spillovers from other regions. In the column, the single central region from the lattice is replaced by a belt of regions around the middle of the column. In the globe there is no inherently central location. The lattice of honeycombs can be considered similar to a country, whereas the globe could be considered representative of the world as a whole. The column can be seen as an intermediate case, since it replaces the one central region of the lattice by a belt of centrally located regions, whereas on the globe every region is centrally located.

The gradual diffusion of knowledge over time and space results in certain equilibrium patterns (that is, patterns which are more or less stable over time) in the distribution of knowledge over regions. In general, these equilibrium patterns show situations in which technological knowledge is unequally distributed over space.

There is a difference in results between the case when the starting value of the knowledge stock is varied and the case in which a parameter is varied across regions. Varying the initial knowledge stock and keeping all parameters equal across regions causes geographic proximity to become the main influence as regions become more equal (that is, as the interval from which the initial values of the knowledge stock are randomly chosen for each region is decreased). Varying a parameter (learning capability or the exogenous rate of knowledge generation) shows that there are two counteracting forces at work. Increasing differences in the parameters are in themselves factors that have a polarizing effect. However, when combined with geographic forces, they lead to less disparity across regions. For example, a region with an unfavourable geographic location may (randomly) obtain a high learning capability, while the centrally located region may (randomly) obtain a low learning capability. In such case, all regions might end up with similar knowledge stocks, since a favourable geographic location leads to more spillovers and therefore a larger growth of the knowledge stock, while a high learning capability (or a high exogenous rate of knowledge generation) also leads to a larger growth of the knowledge stock. Thus, differences in the learning capability or the exogenous rate of growth of the knowledge stock have a net 'adverse' effect on overall disparity.

In the model of Chapter 4, regions were assumed to coexist in a world without national borders. A complete unification of the involved economies prevailed. In fact, no distinction was made between countries. The model in Chapter 6 elaborated the model of Chapter 4 by introducing countries[69] and thereby giving a more adequate representation of reality. This elaboration made it possible to explore the influence of economic integration on the distribution of knowledge and growth across regions.

As before, interregional knowledge spillovers determine the growth of regions. This model is in essence a Goodwin model, as explained in Chapter 3. The model analyses the impact of the different parameters such as the learning capability and the exogenous rate of growth of the knowledge stock on overall disparity across regions in different situations. The impact of barriers to trade was investigated by comparing two different stages of integration. Examining a fixed exchange rate system versus a system of flexible exchange rates resulted in conditions (constellations of parameters) under which fixed exchange rates (compared to flexible exchange rates) generate less disparity across regions. However, depending on the parameter values, fixed exchange rates may also generate more disparity, leading to the conclusion that the effect of monetary integration is ambiguous.

In addition, barriers to knowledge spillovers were considered in the sense that cross-border knowledge flows were hampered compared to inter-country flows. This resulted in a situation where reduced cross-border flows have a large impact when regions are initially unequal with respect to the exogenous rate of growth of knowledge generation or the learning capability. In these cases, the resulting trends in overall disparity are quite different from the trends established in a situation with no barriers to knowledge spillovers.

The most important outcome of this last experiment is that the resulting pattern of per capita gaps shows a clear difference between countries. One of the two countries contains the leader region and this region is located

---

[69] In the simulations two countries are considered; however, the theoretical model allows for *n* countries ($n \geq 2$).

centrally within this country. All other regions of the leader country are grouped in a hierarchical pattern around the central region. The other country contains regions that have a large gap towards the world-leader region. This indicates that, with limited cross-border spillovers, the 'adverse' effect of variety in learning capability and exogenous rate of growth of the knowledge stock, as was demonstrated in Chapter 5, only holds within a country.

The focus of Chapter 7 was to relate the model developed in Chapters 4 and 6 to the present situation in Europe. In this chapter European regional data were explored in order to investigate to what extent the empirically observed patterns resemble those generated by the model. Chapter 7 showed that the distribution of GDP per capita across European regions displays an unequal distribution across space. This is in line with the equilibrium patterns that resulted from the model. The clustering of economic activity was explicitly studied. By using the technique of spatial autocorrelation, the degree to which the value of a variable in one region is spatially correlated to the value in neighbouring regions was assessed. It was shown that regions with a high GDP per capita are surrounded by regions with a similar level of GDP per capita, that is, clustering occurs. This is what is expected on the basis of the predictions of the model.

The models in Chapters 4 and 6 assumed that differences across regions in the exogenous rate of growth of the knowledge stock and learning capability are important for the equilibrium distribution of per capita gaps. Chapter 7 illustrated that these parameters are concentrated within European regions by using R&D data as an indicator. This suggests that differences in these parameters do indeed exist across European regions. Overall, the empirical analysis seems to suggest that an explanation of the distribution of GDP per capita over regions based on knowledge spillovers, knowledge generation and learning capability has some plausibility.

In addition, it was found that variables like population density and higher education R&D are correlated to the R&D of a region. Finally it was shown that the long-run distribution of learning capability and the exogenous rate of growth of the knowledge stock points to the fact that differences across regions in learning capability and exogenous rate of growth of the knowledge stock persist over time.

Chapter 8 was also devoted to illustrating the current situation in Europe with respect to the location and the distribution of economic and innovative activity. However, this chapter took a more distanced stance from the model in that it refrained from the expectations based on the model. In this respect, the chapter directed attention to sector differences (which were assumed to be absent in the model), by exploring data on manufacturing value added and patents.

The general finding was that regions with a large geographic concentration of patents are associated with a large concentration of value added[70]. However, innovative activity is more geographically concentrated than value added. This result might indicate the presence of some sort of increasing returns to location as well as increasing returns to knowledge.

From a sectoral perspective, clear evidence is found of geographic concentrations of innovative as well as economic activity. For most sectors, technological and economic variables are concentrated to a larger extent than population. This is seen when Europe as a whole is observed. In addition, results for the individual countries show that the geographic concentration within sectors is even more profound than at the country level. The extent to which geographic concentration is important differs across sectors, indicating that industry-specific as well as country-specific conditions determine the spatial pattern of innovation and production.

In addition, this chapter attempted to investigate whether spillover effects occur in economic and innovative activity, by using the technique of spatial autocorrelation. In this way it could be investigated whether economic or innovative activity clusters geographically which might suggest the presence of spillover effects. The results indicated that such spillover effects do take place for both types of activity in several sectors. Especially innovative activity shows a large degree of spatial autocorrelation in the majority of sectors, mainly low-tech and medium-tech sectors. High-tech sectors, however, are found to be highly concentrated in few regions, which are not contiguous.

The evidence for spillover effects seems to suggest that locally bounded knowledge spillovers and agglomeration economies play an important role. Furthermore, since innovative and economic concentrations are largely located in the same regions, it seems to be the case that both activities reinforce each other. This observation opens possibilities for future research (see Section 3).

2. POLICY IMPLICATIONS

From a policy perspective, this book provides several interesting insights that can be broadly divided under three headings. First, what do the findings

---

[70] This is in accordance with findings in other empirical studies on this issue, such as Paci and Usai (1998).

imply for regional gaps? Second, how can policy influence the parameter values of the developed model? Third, what are the consequences of several stages of economic integration for disparity across regions?

2.1 Convergence or divergence across European regions

Since European economies have committed themselves to reach a monetary union in the not too distant future, a lot of attention is being directed towards the question of how to achieve convergence across European regions. For policy-makers it is important to know whether regions within the EU are converging or diverging. Divergence across regions exposes a task for the governments to provide economic support for the backward regions. Backward regions can be stimulated to catch up in several ways. In this respect, the European Commission has developed several programmes. Examples of these are Regional Technology Plans (RTPs) and Regional Innovation and Technology Strategy (RITS). The aim of such projects is to stimulate research and development within backward regions and thereby increase the GDP per capita of such a region.

The empirical findings in Chapter 7 and 8 confirm the divergence across regions with respect to economic activity as well as innovative activity. Results in Chapter 7 suggested that, based on the present distribution, divergence in innovation would continue to exist. Therefore, some regions might have locked into a low productivity ~ low innovation situation, while others endure high economic and innovative activity. The model developed in Chapters 4 and 6 suggests that increasing returns to location together with the presence of spillover effects are at the root of this pattern. Region-specific policies might strengthen a weak position of a region by increasing the learning capability and knowledge generation of a region. In this respect the government could stimulate backward regions by providing an efficient knowledge infrastructure. Increasing the attractiveness of a backward region for firms can be reached by means of geographically locating higher education in such a region. However, the question always posed in this context is whether this is an effective course to be followed. As can be concluded from regressions performed in Chapter 7, a clear relationship exists between the presence of higher education in a region and the amount of business R&D performed in that same region. This suggests that the presence of higher education has a positive influence on the location of firms, although the causality between the two works in both ways. This observation is confirmed by studies of Jaffe (1989), Acs, Audretsch and Feldman (1992) and Anselin, Varga and Acs (1997) concerning the effect of academic research on inventions in geographically close private firms.

On the other hand, the findings in Chapter 8 suggest that National Systems of Innovation (NSIs) still have a large influence on the regional patterns in GDP per capita gaps and knowledge. This might be an encouragement to European policy-makers to stimulate a European system of innovation, that is, to improve the knowledge infrastructure within Europe as a whole. It might be useful to set up projects that aim at stimulating the interaction between European universities and research institutes[71].

Chapter 8 increased the awareness of the presence of sectoral clusters, meaning that industries in a specific sector tend to cluster geographically. From a policy perspective, it might be interesting to stimulate the various sectoral clusters and broaden them in spatial terms. This could be done by facilitating economic and knowledge spillovers between the centres of the clusters and the regions surrounding them. This should be combined with a support for public infrastructure in the economically backward regions, as was indicated by Chapter 7, since this might make these regions ready to receive and develop the knowledge and the economic development that will spill over to them when it is their time to border upon an innovative and/or economic cluster.

2.2 Influencing the learning capability and the exogenous rate of knowledge generation

The model developed in this book incorporates at least two parameters that can be influenced by policy. Section 2.1 already gave some suggestions in this respect. First, the learning capability of a region can be influenced by actively trying to enhance the knowledge infrastructure of a region. Stimulating co-operation between firms and research organizations, and ameliorating the educational structure, are measures that have this effect. However, from the simulation results in this study it appears that the existence of differences across regions may not be as 'bad' as is generally believed. The mere existence of differences in learning capabilities across regions may mean that the overall disparity between regions is relatively small.

Second, the exogenous rate of growth of the knowledge stock of a region could be enhanced by stimulating R&D activities in a region. In fact, several

---

[71] See Caracostas and Soete (1997) for an overview of European initiatives that have been undertaken to set up institutions which try to promote interactions of the European Union member states with respect to the innovation process.

policy measures aim at stimulating (private) R&D. Again, the developed model points out that small differences across regions in their exogenous rate of growth of the knowledge stock may lead to relatively large differences across regions with respect to gaps in the knowledge stock.

2.3 Stages of economic integration

In the recent literature, a discussion takes place about whether economic integration, more precisely a monetary union, will have overall positive or negative effects on the growth of the economies involved. Recent developments show that politicians of European countries have made up their minds in this respect and are proceeding with introducing a monetary union.

In Chapter 6, several stages of integration were considered. Regional growth differentials were examined in a situation of flexible exchange rates and compared to a fixed exchange rate system[72]. As said above (Section 1), no unconditional conclusion can be given as to whether the introduction of a monetary union will reduce the overall disparity across regions. The resulting disparity in regional growth depends on the specific characteristics of the regions with respect to factors such as learning capability and exogenous rate of knowledge generation as well as the individual level of the knowledge stocks of the regions involved.

Concerning barriers to knowledge spillovers, the trends in overall disparity are different from the trends found when there are no barriers to knowledge spillovers. This is particularly the case when initial differences across regions increase with respect to their exogenous rate of knowledge generation or their learning capability. Instead of leading to lower overall disparity, pathways of increased overall disparity appear. This could possibly be remedied by policy interaction directed towards taking down those barriers which are still present. Promoting a European System of Innovation would be a good step in this direction (see Chapter 8).

3. FUTURE RESEARCH

The model developed in this book contributes to the existing literature in several ways. It is one of the few attempts in the literature until now to model regional knowledge spillovers. The model incorporates increasing returns to

---

[72] In the model, a system of fixed exchange rates means that each currency can be denominated in the currency of another country against a fixed rate. Therefore, in terms of the model a system of fixed exchange rates is identical to a monetary union.

knowledge as well as increasing returns to location. Furthermore, it is a multi-region ~ multi-country model, which makes it applicable to all countries or groups of countries.

The model can be developed further in several ways. According to the regional interpretation of the Verdoorn~Kaldor law and cumulative causation (Chapter 2), productivity growth will lead to growth in (R&D) investment and, in turn, growth in R&D investment will induce growth in productivity. Therefore, it is reasonable to assume a feedback link from GDP per capita gaps towards innovative activity. This relationship is confirmed by the empirical results from Chapter 7. In this chapter regional GDP per capita was found to be correlated to R&D efforts. It would be interesting to model this feedback from economic activity to innovative activity. A possible result of such an extension could be that such a system reinforces itself to an even larger extent than it does without the feedback link. Probably, regions will sooner find themselves in a situation of low growth accompanied by low innovation. And because both factors (low growth and low innovation) imply that such a region will receive only few spillovers, even from direct neighbours, the backward position of such a region is reinforced. This might induce the even larger task for policy to reverse this vicious low growth / low productivity / low innovativity cycle by stimulating backward regions to strengthen their technological infrastructure and undertake initiatives promoting innovative activity.

Another possible extension of the present study is that the model could be tested against 'real' data. The geographic spheres could easily be replaced by the regional structure of Europe (in fact this was already done in Chapters 7 and 8) or any other group of regions. In order to develop an indicator for learning capability, one could make use of regional data on education. For the exogenous rate of knowledge generation, input or output data of innovative activity can be employed. In this respect, it might also be interesting to compare results for Europe with findings for the United States.

With respect to the empirical analysis, we ran into the problem that regional data were not collected by European institutes until recently. This limits the analysis to descriptive statistics. No time series were available to give a more profound analysis of the underlying mechanisms, and therefore the findings only allow for some speculation on these underlying economic mechanisms. It would be very useful to extend the analysis as soon as time series are available. In this way the evolution over time of clustering of economic and innovative activity could be investigated in more detail. A point which was not considered in this book is that after a certain period of positive externalities to location there might appear diseconomies of agglomeration. Congestion effects might occur. Time series might give some indication of the growth and decline of clusters within Europe.

With further research, knowledge on local knowledge spillovers will increase. This might lead to the application of policy instruments that enhance prosperity and economic stability of regions.

References

Abramovitz, M. (1979), 'Rapid growth potential and its realization: the experience of capitalist economies in the postwar period', in E. Malinvaud (ed.), *Economic Growth and Resources, Vol. I*, London and NewYork: The Macmillan Press.

Abramovitz, M. (1986), 'Catching up, forging ahead, and falling behind', *Journal of Economic History*, **46**, pp. 385~406.

Acs, Z.J., D.B. Audretsch and M.P. Feldman (1992), 'Real effects of academic research: comment', *American Economic Review*, **82**(1), pp. 363~7.

Acs, Z.J., D.B. Audretsch and M.P. Feldman (1993), 'Innovation and R&D spillovers', *CEPR Discussion Paper,* no. 865.

Acs, Z.J., F. Fitzroy and I. Smith (1994), 'High technology employment and university R&D spillovers: Evidence from US cities', CIBER research paper, no. 50.

Allen, P.M. and M. Sanglier (1978), 'Dynamic models in urban growth', *Journal of Social Biological Structures*, **1**, pp. 265~80.

Allen, P.M. and M. Sanglier (1979a), 'A dynamic model of urban growth II', *Journal of Social Biological Structures*, **2**, pp. 269~78.

Allen, P.M. and M. Sanglier (1979b), 'A dynamic model of growth in a central place system', *Geographical Analysis*, **11**(3), pp. 256~72.

Allen, P.M. and M. Sanglier (1981a), 'A dynamic model of a central place system II', *Geographical Analysis*, **13**(2), pp. 149~64.

Allen, P.M. and M. Sanglier (1981b), 'A dynamic model of a central place system III, the effects of trade barriers', *Journal of Social Biological Structures*, **4**, pp. 263~75.

Almeida, P. and B. Kogut (1996), The economic sociology of the geographic localization of ideas and the mobility of patent holders', Wharton School discussion paper.

Ames, E. and N. Rosenberg (1963), 'Changing technological leadership and industrial growth', *Economic Journal*, **73**, pp. 13~31.

Amiti, M. (1998), 'New trade theories and industrial location in the EU: A survey of evidence', *Oxford Review of Economic Policy*, **14**(2), pp. 45~53.

Anselin, L., A. Varga and Z.J. Acs (1997), 'Local geographic spillovers between university research and high technology innovations', *Journal of*

Urban Economics, **42**, pp. 422~48.

Aoki, M. (1986), 'Horizontal vs vertical information structure of the firm', *American Economic Review*, **76**(5), pp. 971~83.

Arthur, W.B. (1988), 'Competing technologies: an overview', in G. Dosi, C. Freeman, R. Nelson, G. Silverberg and L. Soete (eds), *Technical Change and Economic Theory*, London: Pinter Publishers, pp. 590~606.

Arthur, W.B. (1990), 'Urban systems and historical path dependence', in J. Ausubel and R. Herman (eds), *Cities and Their Vital Systems*, Washington D.C.: National Academy Press, pp. 85~97.

Audretsch, D.B. (1995), 'Innovation, growth and survival', *International Journal of Economic Organisation*, **13**, pp. 441~57.

Audretsch, D.B. (1998), 'Agglomeration and the location of innovative activity', *Oxford Review of Economic Policy*, **14**(2), pp. 18~29.

Audretsch, D.B. and M.P. Feldman (1994), 'Knowledge spillovers and the geography of innovation and production', CEPR discussion paper, no. 953.

Audretsch, D.B. and M.P. Feldman (1996), 'Knowledge spillovers and the geography of innovation and production', *American Economic Review*, **86**(3), pp. 630~40.

Balassa, B. (ed.) (1975), *European economic integration*, Amsterdam: North Holland.

Baptista, R. and P. Swann (1998), 'Do firms in clusters innovate more?', *Research Policy*, **27**, pp. 525~40.

Barro, R.J. (1984), *Macroeconomics*, New York: Wiley.

Barro, R.J. (1991), 'Economic growth in a cross section of countries', *Quarterly Journal of Economics*, **106**, pp. 407~43.

Barro, R.J. and X. Sala-i-Martin (1991), 'Convergence across states and regions', *Brooking Papers of Economic Activity*, **1**, pp. 107~82.

Barro, R.J. and X. Sala-i-Martin (1992a), 'Convergence', *Journal of Political Economy*, **100**, pp. 223~51.

Barro, R.J. and X. Sala-i-Martin (1992b), 'Regional growth and migration: A Japan~United States comparison', *Journal of the Japanese and International Economies*, **6**, pp. 312~46.

Barro, R.J. and X. Sala-i-Martin (1995), *Economic Growth*, New York: McGraw-Hill.

Basberg, B. (1987), 'Patents and the measurement of technological change: a survey of the literature', *Research Policy*, **16**, pp. 131~41.

Baumol, W. (1986), 'Productivity growth, convergence and welfare: What the long-run data show', *American Economic Review*, **76**, pp. 1072~85.

Baumol, W., S.A. Batey Blackman and E. Wolff (1989), *Productivity and*

American Leadership: The Long View, Cambridge, MA and London: The MIT Press.

Borts, G.H. (1960), 'The equalization of returns and regional economic growth', *The American Economic Review*, pp. 319~47.

Borts, G.H. and J.L. Stein (1964), *Economic Growth in a Free Market*, New York: Columbia University Press.

Boschma, R.A. (1994), *Looking through a Window of Locational Opportunity. A long term spatial analysis of techno-industrial upheavals in Great Britain and Belgium*, Tinbergen Institute Research Series, no. 75, Amsterdam: Thesis Publishers.

Boschma, R.A. and B. van der Knaap (1997), 'New technology and windows of locational opportunity: indeterminacy, creativity and chance', in Reijnders (ed.), *Economics and Evolution*, Aldershot: Edward Elgar.

Boudeville, J.R. (1966), *Problems of Regional Economic Planning*, Edinburgh: Edinburgh University Press.

Breschi, S. (1995), 'Spatial patterns of innovation: evidence from patent data', paper presented at the workshop on 'New Research Findings: The Economics of Scientific and Technological Research in Europe', Urbino, Italy, 24-25 February 1995.

Brown, L.A. (1981), *Innovation Diffusion, a New Perspective*, London and New York: Methuen.

Buswell, R.J. and E.W. Lewis (1970) 'The geographical distribution of industrial research activity in the United Kingdom', *Regional Studies*, **4**, pp. 297~306.

Caracostas, P. and L. Soete, (1997), 'The building of post-national institutions in Europe', in C. Edquist (ed.), *Systems of Innovation: Technologies, Institutions and Organizations*, London: Pinter/Cassell Academic.

Christaller, W. (1933), *Central Places in Southern Germany*, Englewood Cliffs and New York: Prentice Hall.

Cliff, A.D. and J.K. Ord (1973), *Spatial Autocorrelation*, London: Pion Limited.

Coe, D.T., and E. Helpman (1995), 'International R&D spillovers', *European Economic Review*, **39**, pp. 859~87.

Cohen, W.M. and D.A. Levinthal (1989), 'Innovation and learning: The two faces of R&D', *Economic Journal*, **99**, pp. 569~96.

Coombs, R., P. Saviotti and V. Walsh (1987), *Economics and Technological Change*, London: Macmillan.

Cowan, R. and D. Foray (1997), 'The economics of codification and the diffusion of knowledge', *Industrial and Corporate Change*, **6**(3), pp. 595~622.

Darwent, D.F. (1969), 'Growth poles and growth centres in regional planning: a review', *Environment and Planning*, **1**, pp. 5~31.

Dasgupta, P. and P.A. David (1993), 'Toward a new economics of science', revision of the paper presented at the Center for Economic Policy Research Conference, Stanford, 1992.

David, P. (1975), *Technical Choice, Innovation and Economic Growth*, Cambridge: Cambridge University Press.

Davies, S. (1979), *The Diffusion of Process Innovations*, Cambridge: Cambridge University Press.

Day, R.H. (1970), 'A theoretical note on the spatial diffusion of something new', *Geographical Analysis*, **2**, pp. 68~76.

De Long, J.B. (1988), 'Productivity growth, convergence and welfare: comment', *American Economic Review*, **78**, pp. 1138~59.

DeBresson, C. and F. Amessa (1991), 'Networks of innovators: A review and introduction to the issue', *Research Policy*, **20**, pp. 363~379.

Dixon, R.J. and A.P. Thirlwall (1975), 'A model of regional growth-rate differences on Kaldorian lines', *Oxford Economic Papers*, **11**, pp. 201~14.

Dorfman, N. (1983), 'Route 128: the development of a regional high-technology economy', *Research Policy*, **12**, pp. 299~316.

Dosi, G. (1988), 'The nature of the innovative process', in Dosi, G., et al. (eds), *Technical Change and Economic Theory*, London: Pinter Publishers, pp. 221~38.

Dosi, G., K. Pavitt and L. Soete (1990), *The Economics of Technical Change and International Trade*, New York: Harvester Wheatsheaf.

Dowrick, S. (1997), 'Trade and growth: a survey', in J. Fagerberg, P. Hansson, L. Lundberg and A. Melchior (eds), *Technology and international trade*, Aldershot: Edward Elgar, pp. 107~26

Durlauf, S.N. and P.A. Johnson (1992), 'Local versus global convergence: across national economies', NBER Working Paper, No. 3996. Cambridge, MA: National Bureau of Economic Research.

Echeverri-Caroll, E.L. and L. Hunnicutt (1997), 'The sources of knowledge for innovations', paper presented at the 37th European Congress of the Regional Science Association, Rome, 1997.

Encyclopaedia Britannica, 1998.

Fagerberg, J. (1988), 'Why growth rates differ', in G. Dosi et al. (eds), *Technical Change and Economic Theory*, London: Pinter Publishers, pp. 432~57.

Fagerberg, J., B. Verspagen and N. von Tunzelman (eds) (1994), *The dynamics of technology, trade and growth*, Aldershot: Edward Elgar.

Feldman, M.P. (1994a), *The Geography of Innovation*, Boston: Kluwer

Academic Press.

Feldman, M.P. (1994b), 'Knowledge complementarity and innovation', *Small Business Economics*, **6**, pp. 363~72.

Feldman, M.P. and D.B. Audretsch (1999), 'Innovation in cities: Science-based diversity, specialization and localized competition', *European Economic Review*, **43**, pp. 409~29.

Feldman, M.P. and R. Florida (1994), 'The geographic sources of innovation: technological infrastructure and product innovation in the United States', *Annals of the Association of American Geographers*, **84**(2), pp. 210~29.

Fischer, R.A. (1930), *The Genetical Theory of Natural Selection*, Oxford: Clarendon Press.

Flam, H. (1992), 'Product markets and 1992: full integration, large gains', *Journal of Economic Perspectives*, **6**, pp. 7~31.

Freeman, C. (1991), 'Networks of innovators: a synthesis of research issues', *Research Policy*, **20**, pp. 499~514.

Friedman, J. (1967), *A General Theory of Polarized Development*, the Ford Foundation, urban and regional advisory programme in Chile, Santiago: Chile.

Gabisch, G. and H.W. Lorenz, (1989), *Business Cycle Theory, a Survey of Methods and Concepts*, Berlin: Springer-Verlag.

Gandolfo, G. (1996), *Economic Dynamics*, Berlin: Springer-Verlag.

Gerschenkron, A. (1962), *Economic Backwardness in Historical Perspective*, Cambridge: The Belknap Press of Harvard University Press.

Gomulka, S. (1971), *Inventive Activity, Diffusion and the Stages of Economic Growth*, Aarhus: Aarhus.

Gomulka, S. (1990), *The Theory of Technological Change and Economic Growth*, London: Routledge.

Goodwin, R.M. (1967), 'A growth cycle', in C.H. Feldstein (ed.), *Socialism, Capitalism and Economic Growth*, London: MacMillan.

Gregersen, B., B. Johnson and A. Kristensen (1994), 'National systems of innovation and European integration'. Paper presented to the EUNETIC Conference on Evolutionary Economics and Technical Change: Assessment of Results and New Frontiers, European Parliament, Strasbourg, 6-8 October.

Gregersen, B. and B. Johnson (1997), 'Learning economies, innovation systems and European integration', *Regional Studies*, **31**(5), pp. 479~90.

Griliches, Z. (1979), 'Issues in assessing the contribution of R&D to productivity growth', *Bell Journal of Economics*, **10**, pp. 92~116.

Griliches, Z. (1990), 'Patent statistics as economic indicators: a survey', *Journal of Economic Literature*, **28**, pp. 1661~707.

Grossman, G. and E. Helpman (1990), 'Trade, innovation and growth',

American Economic Review, **80**(2), pp. 86~92.

Grossman, G. and E. Helpman (1992), *Innovation and Growth in the Global Economy*, Cambridge: MIT Press.

Hägerstrand, T. (1966), *Innovation and Diffusion as a Spatial Process*, Chicago: The university of Chicago Press.

Hagett, P., A.D. Cliff and A. Frey (1977), *Locational Models*, London: Edward Arnold (publishers) Ltd.

Hanson, G.H. (1998), 'North American economic integration and industry location', *Oxford Review of Economic Policy*, **14**(2), pp. 30~43.

Hofbauer, J., and K. Sigmund (1988), *The Theory of Evolution and Dynamical Systems*, Cambridge: Cambridge University Press.

Jaffe, A. (1989), 'Real effects of academic research', *American Economic Review*, **79**, pp. 957~70.

Jaffe, A. (1996), 'Economic analysis of research spillovers, implications for the advanced technology program', paper prepared for the Advanced Technology Program, December 1996.

Jaffe, A., M. Traijtenberg and R. Henderson (1993), 'Geographic localization of knowledge spillovers as evidenced by patent citations', *Quarterly Journal of Economics*, **108**, pp. 577~98.

Jagger, N. and S. Perryman (1996), *Measurement of Employment in High Technology Sectors at the Regional Level*, The Institute for Employment Studies.

Johnson, B. and B. Gregersen (1997), 'European integration and national systems of innovation', European Commission.

Kaldor, N. (1970), 'The case for regional policies', *Scottish Journal of Political Economy*, **17**, pp. 337~47.

Kaldor, N. (1975), 'What is wrong with economic theory', *Quarterly Journal of Economics*, **89**, pp. 347~57.

Kozul-Wright, R. and R. Rowthorn (1998), 'Spoilt for choice? Multinational corporations and the geography of international production', *Oxford Review of Economic Policy*, **14**(2), pp. 74~92.

Krugman, P. (1991), *Economic Geography and Trade*, Cambridge, MA and London: The MIT Press.

Krugman, P. (1996), *The Self-organizing Economy*, Cambridge: Blackwell.

Krugman, P. (1998), 'What's new about the new economic geography?', *Oxford Review of Economic Policy*, **14**(2), pp. 7~17.

Lall, S. (1998), 'Exports of manufactures by developing countries: Emerging patterns of trade and location', *Oxford Review of Economic Policy*, **14**(2), pp. 54~73.

Lorenz, H.W. (1989), *Nonlinear Dynamical Economic Systems and Chaotic*

Motion, Berlin: Springer-Verlag.

Lösch, A. (1954), *The Economics of Location,* translated by W.G. Woglon from 2nd revised edition, New Haven, Conn.: Yale University Press.

Lotka, A.J. (1956), *Elements of Mathematical Biology (*formerly published under the title: *Elements of Physical Biology*, London: Constable, 1925), New York: Dover Publications reprint.

Lucas, R. (1988), 'On the mechanics of economic development', *Journal of Monetary Economics*, **22**, pp. 3~42.

Maddison, A. (1982), *Phases of Capitalist Development*, Oxford and New York: Oxford University Press.

Malecki, E.J. (1980), 'Dimensions of R&D location in the United States', *Research Policy*, **9**, pp. 2~22.

Malecki, E.J (1983), 'Technology and regional development: a survey', *International Regional Science Review*, **8**, pp. 89~125.

Malecki, E.J. and P. Varaiya (1986), 'Innovation and changes in regional structure', in P. Nijkamp (ed.), *Handbook of Regional and Urban Economics*, Amsterdam: North-Holland, Vol. 1, pp. 629~45.

Malerba, F. and L. Orsenigo (1995), 'Schumpeterian patterns of innovation', *Cambridge Journal of Economics*, **19**(1), pp. 47~66.

Mankiw, N.G., D. Romer and D.N. Weil (1992), 'A contribution to the empirics of economic growth', *Quarterly Journal of Economics*, **107**, pp. 407~38.

Mansfield, E. (1968), *The Economics of Technical Change*, New York: W.W. Norton.

Mansfield, E. (1991), 'Academic research and industrial innovation', *Research Policy,* **20**, pp.1~12.

Marshall, A. (1920), *Principles of Economics*, London: MacMillan.

McGrew, J.C. and C.B. Monroe (1993), *An Introduction to Statistical Problem Solving in Geography*, Dubuque, Iowa: Wm. C. Brown Publishers.

Metcalfe, J.S. (1981), 'Impulse and diffusion in the study of technical change', *Futures*, **13**, pp. 347~59.

Metcalfe, J.S. (1988), 'The diffusion of innovation: an interpretative survey', in G. Dosi, C. Freeman, R. Nelson, G. Silverberg and L. Soete (eds), *Technical Change and Economic Theory*, London: Pinter Publishers, pp. 560~89.

Molle, W. (1980), *Regional Disparity and Economic Development in the European Community*, Farnborough, England: Saxon House.

Morgan, K. (1997), 'The learning region: institutions, innovation and regional renewal', *Regional Studies*, **31**(5), pp. 491~503.

Moseley, M.J. (1974), *Growth Centres in Regional Planning*, Oxford:

Pergamon.

Müller, K. and Nejedly (1971/1972), 'The regional distribution of research and development (a note)', *Research Policy*, **1**, pp. 320~28.

Myrdal, G. (1957), *Economic Theory and Under-developed Regions*, London: Gerald Duckworth & Co. LTD.

Nelson, R.R. (1989), 'US technological leadership: where did it come from and where did it go?', pp. 1~45.

Nelson, R.R. and S.G. Winter (1982), *An Evolutionary Theory of Economic Change*, Cambridge, Mass.: Harvard University Press.

Neven, D., and C. Gouyette (1995), 'Regional convergence in the European Community', *Journal of Common Market Studies*, **33**, pp. 47~65.

Ohkawa, K. and H. Rosovsky (1973), *Japanese Economic Growth*, Stanford, CA: Stanford University Press.

Ottaviano, G.I.P. and D. Puga (1997), 'Agglomeration in the global economy: a survey of the "new economic geography"', Centre for Economic Performance Discussion Paper, no. 356.

Paci, R. and S. Usai (1998), 'Technological enclaves and industrial districts, an analysis of the regional distribution of innovative activity in Europe', paper presented at the 38th European Congress of the Regional Science Association, Vienna.

Park, W.G. (1995), 'International R&D spillovers and OECD economic growth', *Economic Inquiry*, **33**(4), pp. 571~91.

Pavitt, K. (1985), 'Patent statistics as indicators of innovation activities', *Scientometrics*, **7**, pp. 77~99.

Pavitt, K. (1987), *On the Nature of Technology*, Brighton: University of Sussex – Science Policy Research Unit.

Pelkmans, J. (1997), *European Integration, Methods and Economic Analysis*, Heerlen: Longman.

Perroux, F. (1955), 'Note sur la notion de pôle de croissance', *Économie Appliquée*, **7**, pp. 307~20, translated in I. Livingstone (ed.) (1971), *Economic Policy for Development*, Baltimore: Penguin, pp. 278~89.

Polanyi, M. (1958), *PersonaL Knowledge: Towards a Post-critical Philosophy*, London: Routledge and Kegan.

Quah, D. (1993), 'Empirical cross-section dynamics in economic growth', *European Economic Review*, **37**, pp. 426~34.

Rauch, J.E. (1993), 'Does history matter only when it matters little? The case of city-industry location', *Quarterly Journal of Economics*, **108**, pp. 843~67.

Richardson, H.W. (1973), *Regional Growth Theory*, London: Macmillan Press.

Richardson, H.W. (1978a), *Regional and Urban Economics*, Hindsdale: Dryden Press.

Richardson, H.W. (1978b), 'The state of regional economics: a survey article', *International Regional Science Review*, **3**, pp. 1~48.

Robson, B.T. (1973), *Urban Growth: an Approach*, London: Methuen & Co.

Romer, P. (1986), 'Increasing returns and long run growth', *Journal of Political Economy*, **94**, pp. 1002~37.

Romer, P. (1990), 'Endogenous technological change', *Journal of Political Economy*, **98**, pp. S71~S102.

Rosegger, G. (1980), *The Economics of Production and Innovation*, New York: Pergamon.

Sargent, T.J. (1993), *Bounded Rationality in Macroeconomics*, Oxford: Clarendon Press.

Saxenian, A. (1985), 'Silicon Valley and Route 128: regional prototypes or historical exceptions?' in M. Castells (ed.), *High Technology, Space and Society*, Beverly Hills: Sage, pp. 81~105.

Scherer, F.M. (1983), 'The propensity to patent', *International Journal of Industrial Organization*, **1**, pp. 107~28.

Schumpeter, J.A. (1928), 'The instability of capitalism', *Economic Journal*, **38**, pp. 361~86.

Schumpeter, J.A. (1934), *The Theory of Economic Development*, Cambridge: Harvard University Press.

Schumpeter, J.A. (1939), *Business Cycles: A Theoretical, Historical and Statistical Analysis, vol. i, vol. ii*, New York: McGraw-Hill.

Schumpeter, J.A. (1943), *Capitalism, Socialism and Democracy*, London: Allen and Unwin.

Scott, A.J. (1988), *New Industrial Spaces: Flexible Production Organisation and Regional Development in North America and Western Europe*, London: Pion.

Siebert, H. (1969), *Regional Economic Growth: Theory and Policy*, Scranton, Pennsylvania: International Textbook Company.

Silverberg, G. (1984), 'Embodied technical progress in a dynamic economic model: the self-organisation paradigm', in R.M. Goodwin, M. Krüger and A. Vercelli (eds), *Non-linear Models of Fluctuating Growth*, Berlin: Springer-Verlag, pp. 192~208.

Silverberg, G. (1988), 'Modelling economic dynamics and technical change: mathematical approaches to self-organisation and evolution', in G. Dosi, C. Freeman, R. Nelson, G. Silverberg and L. Soete (eds), *Technical Change and Economic Theory*, London: Pinter Publishers, pp. 531~59.

Simon, H.A. (1986), 'On the behavioural and rational foundations of economic dynamics', in R.M. Day and G. Eliasson (eds), *The Dynamics of*

Market Economics, Amsterdam: North Holland, pp. 21~44.

Soete, L. and R. Turner (1984), 'Technology diffusion and the rate of technical change', *The Economic Journal*, **94**, pp. 612~23.

Solow, R.M. (1956), 'A contribution to the theory of economic growth', *Quarterly Journal of Economics*, **70**, pp. 65~94.

Solow, R.M. (1970), *Growth Theory: an Exposition*, Oxford: Oxford University Press.

Stiglitz, J.E. (1987), 'Learning to learn, localized learning and technological progress', in P. Dasgupta and P. Stoneman (eds), *Economic Policy and Technological Performance*, Cambridge: Cambridge University Press, pp. 123~53.

Stohr, W. (1986), 'Regional innovation complexes', *Papers of the Regional Science Association*, **59**, pp. 29~44.

Stoneman, P. (1983), *The Economic Analysis of Technological Change*, Oxford: Oxford University Press.

Stoneman, P. (1984), 'Theoretical approaches to the analysis of the diffusion of new technology', in S. MacDonald et al. (eds), *The Trouble with Technology*, London: Frances Pinter.

Storper, M. (1995), 'The resurgence of regional economics, ten years later: the region as a nexus of untraded interdependencies', *European Urban and Regional Studies*, **2**(3), pp. 191~221.

Storper, M. and R. Walker (1989), *The Capitalist Imperative. Territory, Technology and Industrial Growth*, Oxford: Blackwell.

Swan, T.W. (1956), 'Economic growth and capital accumulation', *Economic Record*, **32**, pp. 334~61.

Todd, D. (1974), 'An appraisal of the development pole concept in regional analysis', *Environment and Planning A*, **6**, pp. 291~306.

Ullman, E.L. (1958), 'Regional development and the geography of concentration', *Papers and Proceedings of the Regional Science Association*, **4**, pp. 179~98.

Van der Knaap, B. and W. Sleegers (1995), 'Regional economic development and cohesion in North-West Europe', *Tijdschrift voor Economische en Sociale Geografie*, **86**(3), pp. 296~302.

Verdoorn, P.J. (1949), 'Fattori che regolano lo sviluppo della produttiva del lavoro' (Factors governing the growth of labour productivity), *L'industria*, **1**, pp. 3~10 (English translation: A.P. Thirlwall and G. Thirlwall (eds) (1979), *Research in Population and Economics*).

Verspagen, B. (1991), 'A new empirical approach to catching up and falling behind', *Structural Change and Economic Dynamics*, **2**, pp. 359~80.

Verspagen, B. (1992a), 'Endogenous innovation in neo-classical growth models: a survey', *Journal of Macroeconomics*, **14**, pp. 631~62.

Verspagen, B. (1992b), *Uneven Growth Between Interdependent Economies: an Evolutionary View on Technology Gaps, Trade and Growth*, Maastricht: Datawyse.

Verspagen, B. (1997), 'European regional clubs: do they exist, and where are they heading? On economic and technological differences between European regions', paper presented at the 3rd Conference on 'Economic Growth and Change, A Comparative Analysis', Cagliari, Italy, June 19-21, 1997.

Verspagen, B., T. van Moergastel and M. Slabbers (1994), 'MERIT concordance table: IPC – ISIC (rev. 2)', MERIT Research Memorandum, no. 2/94~004.

Volterra, V. (1927), 'Variazioni e fluttuazioni del numero díndividui in specie animali convivemto', in *Memorie del R. Comitato talassografico italiano, memoria CXXXI*, reprinted in V. Volterra (1962), Opere mathematiche: memorie e note, Rome: Áccademia Nazionale dei Lincei, Vol. V, pp. 1~106.

Von Hippel, E. (1988), *The Sources of Innovation*, New York: Oxford University Press.

Von Hippel, E. (1994), '"Sticky information" and the locus of problem solving: implications for innovation', *Management Science*, **40**(3), pp. 429~39.

Von Thünen, J.H. (1826), *Der isolierte Staat in Beziehung auf Landwirtschaft und Nationalökonomie*, Hamburg.

Index

Abramovitz, M. 9, 17, 18, 185
Acs, Z.J. 3, 28, 180, 185, 186
agglomeration 4, 27, 28, 130, 174,
  184
  economies 14, 15, 29, 40, 42, 169,
  179
Allen, P.M. 40, 185, 193
Almeida, P. 3, 28, 185
Ames, E. 19, 185
Amessa, F. 188
Anselin, L. 180, 186
Aoki, M. 26, 186
applied research 23
Arthur, W.B. 34, 35, 40, 186
Audretsch, D.B. 3, 4, 5, 8, 9, 26, 28,
  157, 163, 180, 185, 186, 189

Balassa, B. 84, 186
Baptista, R. 3, 186
barriers to knowledge spillovers 7,
  82, 83, 84, 85, 102, 103, 106,
  107, 108, 110, 112, 113, 115,
  160, 177, 182
Barro, R.J. 11, 12, 44, 186
Basberg, B. 150, 186
basic research 3, 23, 24
Batey Blackman, S.A. 187
Baumol, W. 19, 20, 44, 187
bifurcation 49, 50, 53
biology 32, 33, 35, 191
  biological evolution 34
Borts, G.H. 8, 10, 12, 187
Boschma, R.A. 25, 187
Boudeville, J.R. 14, 187
bounded rationality 31
Breschi, S. 4, 5, 28, 152, 187
Brown, L.A. 22, 187, 191
Buswell, R.J. 28, 187

Caracostas, P. 181, 187
catch-up 1, 17, 18, 19, 20, 43, 44, 45,
  46, 47, 48, 49, 52, 55, 56, 64,
  65, 71, 76, 176, 180, 195
  parameter 51
Christaller, W. 27, 187
Cliff, A.D. 59, 119, 120, 164, 187,
  190
clustering 4, 9, 26, 27, 28, 119, 121,
  159, 164, 165, 166, 178, 183
clusters 3, 10, 14, 15, 25, 27, 28, 40,
  166, 179, 181, 184, 186
Coe, D.T. 20, 187
Cohen, W.M. 127, 187
communication 1, 3, 4, 8, 14, 23, 27,
  40, 166
  flows 24, 84
competitiveness 35, 88, 91
convergence 11, 12, 18, 19, 98, 137,
  138, 169, 180, 187, 188, 192
  local 20
Coombs, R. 17, 31, 187
Cowan, R. 8, 188
cross-border spillovers 114, 178
cumulative causation 10, 12, 13, 15,
  34, 40, 174, 183

Darwent, D.F. 21, 188
Darwin, 32, 33
Dasgupta, P. 4, 188, 194
David, P.A. 4, 9, 16, 188
Davies, S. 188
Day, R.H. 23, 188, 194
De Long, J.B. 19, 20, 44, 188
DeBresson, C. 188
diffusion
  general spatial diffusion model 21
  hierarchical 21, 22
  imperfect 174
  knowledge 6, 8, 9, 10, 13, 16, 20,
  21, 84, 117, 174, 176, 188
  model 21, 22
disembodied knowledge spillovers 6,